BUILDING
WITH THE END
IN MIND

A Complete Succession Planning
Guide for Professional Service Owners

DAVID GRAU SR., JD

Building With The End In Mind
A Complete Succession Planning Guide for Professional Service Owners

Paperback ISBN: 979-8-9912629-7-2
Hardcover ISBN: 979-8-9912629-8-9
Audiobook ISBN: 979-8-9912629-6-5

Business Transitions Publishing, LLC
Lexington, KY
Printed in the United States of America

OTHER BOOKS BY DAVID GRAU SR., JD,

The Stewardship Advantage
Building a Profitable and Principled Small Business –
with the Power to Change the World! (2025)

Acquiring Your Future Through a Succession Plan:
A Primer for Next Gen Professional Service Providers (2025)

Buying, Selling, and Valuing Financial Practices (2016)

Succession Planning for Financial Advisors:
Building an Enduring Business (2014)

This book is dedicated to that intrepid group of Professional Service owners who are willing to consider and support a changing of the guard to the next generation. I appreciate in advance your flexibility, confidence, and perseverance during this detailed and often thought-provoking exploration of Succession Planning.

TABLE OF CONTENTS

YOUR GUIDE

I am putting this section up front because I want you to know who your guide is.

In the course of authoring this book, I read all the published and self-published authors in this succession planning genre. Frankly, as applied to a professional services practice, I must conclude that many succession planning authors lack a true understanding of the complex details and unique benefits involved in the actual succession planning process. I am not one of them.

In the world of small businesses owned and operated by professional service owners (as I define such terms below in the Introduction section), succession planning is not the same thing as selling your entire business to a key employee, family member, or outside buyer, and walking away. The succession plans that we will explore in this book are all about *gradual ownership transition*. The plans I have worked on for the past 25+ years involve one or more founders who sell their equity, incrementally, to one or more next generation buyers who buy the founder's shares at Fair Market Value and pay for the opportunity over time even as they work full time to help grow the very business in which they have invested. These plans are designed to last for a lifetime. It is the opposite of a onetime event.

I am schooled in the law, securities regulation, business taxation, entity design and structure, and business building. These are the gears in the machinery that I enjoy working on. I started small and built and learned, like many other professional service owners. Prior to semi-retirement, I was an owner in a professional services business with sixty-five employees, complete with a multi-million dollar annual payroll, a Marketing Team and a Sales Team, a Line of Credit, a full-time bookkeeping staff, and so on. In this dynamic small business, we *cracked the code* on succession planning and helped professional service owners design and implement the plans addressed in this book. Along the way, I designed and built an open marketplace for financial service professionals to sell their practices in an organized manner to a third-party and today, a profession that had little if any ascertainable value just 25 years ago, enjoys a 50:1 buyer to seller ratio that supports the highest value of any professional services model, so far. This first, crucial step helped to power the succession planning that followed.

Prior to all that, I was a sole proprietor in my own law practice. In the beginning, I was a force of one, *hanging out my shingle* and starting in the same place as many of you. I *loved* being a sole proprietor! In truth, at least for the first couple of years, I owned *a job* that depended entirely on me to generate income, handle marketing, sales, customer service, and more. If things didn't go well, I could have a heart-to-heart talk with the owner every morning. But things got better and grew and I added some much needed help.

In time, I sold my small law practice and used the money to start a professional services business specializing in succession planning, exit planning and continuity planning, an operation that provided hundreds of business valuations every year (over 15,000 by the time I *kind of* retired). Twenty-five years later, I completed my own succession plan, selling my equity incrementally back to the business I started and to the next generation owners, all of whom I hired directly or indirectly. And then that business continued on without me, and that completed the circle...up to that point.

Looking back, I very much enjoyed both careers. I also learned first-hand the difference between owning a job, owning a practice, and owning a business. They are not the same and it matters a lot, because where you begin your journey impacts where and how you might end it.

Over the past 25 years, I led well over five hundred specific, detailed, personal succession planning consulting engagements, as well as speaking to audiences and conducting workshops that cumulatively total thousands more plan participants, each working through one or more tranches (something you will learn about in Lesson No. 6). Some of the plans I consulted on and helped to design were small practices with just one or two owners, often a parent and a son or daughter; others were fairly large, with 20 owners from multiple generations. Valuations for these practices and businesses ranged from $500,000 to over $50 million—but most were in the $2,000,000 to $15,000,000 range. In the professional services world, this is what I know.

I have had two previous books published on this subject matter. In 2014, I wrote my first book, titled *Succession Planning for Financial Advisors/Building an Enduring Business,* published by Wiley & Sons/ Wiley Finance Series. In 2016, I wrote a companion book titled *Buying, Selling and Valuing Financial Practices*, also published by Wiley & Sons. Both books are still relevant and available on Amazon. Prior to authoring these books, I authored a monthly column in *Financial Planning Magazine* for six years on the subjects of succession planning, business perpetuation, and valuation. I have written and published two dozen professional white papers, have won a host of awards, graced a magazine cover or two, and been the subject of numerous articles for my contributions and thought leadership.

I put this section up front because I want you to know who your guide is, and is not, and I need you to understand that I know what I am doing. I am honored that you are reading this book and allowing me to try to make a real difference in your business and work life.

A FOUR-PART INTRODUCTION:

As a professional reader, I often skip over the Introduction unless I really like the book, and then I go back and read the Introduction afterwards. Sometimes books are so great that I don't want to leave them and reading the Introduction section at the end gives me an excuse to hold on to it, and connect with the author, for a few minutes more. Whatever you end up thinking about this book, I implore you not to skip this multi-part Introduction before reading the fifty Lessons. It is not fluff. This is a mechanical, prescriptive, non-fiction book and the instructions start right here, right now. This is where we start gathering the tools to put in our toolbox for our later work.

PART ONE OF THE INTRODUCTION - A SENSE OF PERSPECTIVE.

One of the most important questions I ask of a client who is considering a succession plan is this: "How do you see your story ending?" This is a question well worth pondering from day one of an entrepreneur's career. When you start a journey, shouldn't you have a clear idea of where, and approximately when, you would like it to end?

Every entrepreneur and business owner has a dream. Every owner has an idea of how they would like their story to end. Entrepreneurs were born to dream big and set lofty goals. I learned from experience that what you do along the way, starting years even decades before you think about retirement, starting now, perhaps, will provide more options and better choices when it comes time to completely and finally answer the question in a way that satisfies you and your family, your key employees, and your clients. So, what is your answer to that question? That is why this book has been written.

As your guide, I have stood at the base of the business-building mountain looking up, and decades later, I've stood on the summit looking back down. No one completes the perfect, unscathed trek, and some mountain tops are higher than others, but everyone can learn from those who have gone before them. In this book, I would like to provide you with a sense of perspective. I will pause now and then in the pages that follow, as we work through the Lessons, and do a "Quick aside," like a breather, or a deep sigh as we take a moment to look around and collect our thoughts. We will take the opportunity to *reset the table* on occasion and get things in order before proceeding. Complicated is one path; knowledgeable, confident, and comfortable is yet another. I'll guide you on the latter path during our journey.

This book is not about selling your business and walking away—this is a drum I am going to beat incessantly. Succession planning is about building something bigger than you and empowering the people you have surrounded yourself with. It is about selling, in most cases, to a successor *team* who buys your equity incrementally over the years, sometimes decades. These buyers are investors in the business you're building!

There are some important Lessons in this book that will help you build a better, more valuable business. That said, sole proprietorships, practices, and small businesses with little growth or profitability and the inability or unwillingness to change that course will not survive the first generation of ownership. A multiple-owner, multiple-generational business requires a strong, purposely built foundation that supports value, and is profitable, growing, and investable, as I will explain further. However your story ends, conquering these elements will give you better and more lucrative choices when you start to stare down that inevitable, impatient point on the horizon.

If you have spent any time looking into the subject of succession planning, you have probably read that the odds are against you and not many founding owners succeed in transitioning their businesses to a second generation of ownership, let alone a third generation. My experience is that most attempts to implement a succession plan fail not because the process is too hard or too demanding on the participants, but because the founding generation of ownership starts too late, hasn't constructed the business elements correctly, doesn't understand the issues specific to a *professional services* succession plan, and listens to a lot of bad or inexperienced advice along the way. Let's start to solve those problems right now because the choices and solutions most certainly lie within your control, if you build with the end in mind.

PART TWO OF THE INTRODUCTION - WHAT IS A PROFESSIONAL SERVICES BUSINESS?

The term "Professional Services," at least for the purposes of the succession planning strategies referred to in this book, includes any practice or business whose core output is a service requiring specialized knowledge or skill and often requiring a professional degree, license, certification or registration. A key aspect of Professional Services is providing solutions to problems encountered by individuals and businesses. Examples of Professional Services include:

Accounting and Tax Practices	Doctors and Medical Groups
Acting Coaches/Workshops	Engineering Services
Advertising and Marketing Agencies	Environmental Technology
Analytics Services	Event Management
Architectural Firms	Financial Services/ Wealth Management
Bookkeeping Services	HR Firms
Business Valuation Firms	Independent Insurance Professionals
Consulting Firms	
Contractors (Electrical, Mechanical, etc.)	IT Services/Computer Science
Creative Agencies	Legal Services/Law Firms
Dental Services	Logistics and Transportation
	Media & Entertainment

Payroll Services

Public Relations Firms

Publishing/Writing Services

Real Estate Brokerages

Research & Development

Software & Information Technology

Speech Pathologists

Storage Service Providers

Systems Integration Services

Technology Consultants

Physical Therapists

Travel, Tourism & Hospitality

Web Developers and Designers

...and the list goes on. I have even worked with an off-Broadway production company and a Hollywood studio, among others. These Professional Service owners and providers face unique challenges when it comes to perpetuating the work that they do, but they also have some distinct advantages.

Hopefully it is apparent that with so many types of Professional Services offered there will be vast differences in how practices or businesses operate in terms of overhead expenses, professional compensation, growth rates, and profitability. There will be Professional Service businesses that generate 40% to 50% profitability, or EBITDA, while others will work every bit as hard and take all the risks to bring just 8% to 12% to the *bottom line* after everything and everyone has been paid. Many consultants write that this is just the way it is, but we'll show you how to push back on this front. Regardless, a well-designed succession plan can work well at both ends of the performance spectrum.

PART THREE OF THE INTRODUCTION - THE INTENDED AUDIENCE FOR THIS BOOK.

This book is written for Professional Service providers, as defined above, most of whom will be first generation owners, or G1s, with a staff of many, or at least a few. Other readers may be involved in working as a force of one, a sole proprietorship, or a book builder. *Individual* Professional Service providers are not really the intended audience for this book unless you are building something larger or are interested in buying into or merging into a larger Professional Services business. That said, even individual Professional Service providers can add value and strength to their work through the Lessons in this book and, one day, even perpetuate your own line of work.

Fine tuning this general approach, consider that this book is applicable to Professional Service owners and providers who fit these parameters:

(a) One or more owners of a business entity (such as an LLC or corporation) providing or supporting the delivery of Professional Services

(b) Current W2 employees who aspire to purchase an ownership interest in the practice or business where they work

(c) Family businesses or, more commonly, family-like businesses that depend on more than just blood relatives to make it all work and last

(d) Practices or businesses with a minimum annual gross revenue of $500,000, up to around $20,000,000. Note that I am not citing anyone's definition of a small business here; I am merely relating my actual experiences in setting up succession plans for this size and type of profession.

(e) Professional Service businesses with up to a total of fifty people, including owners

(f) The lawyers, accountants, bankers, family members, or insurance agents whose role is to provide counsel to anyone in the preceding categories who wants to create a legacy.

Note that there is a second book in this series specifically for next generation owners or ownership prospects in a larger, first generation business. Next generation owners and prospects face unique challenges and needs, which are not covered in this book. This second companion book, to be published in February 2025 under the working title *Acquiring Your Future Through a Succession Plan: A Primer for Next Generation Professional Service Providers*, is already underway. As you will learn, most succession plans require two or more up-and-coming professional service providers per business, which means we collectively need to help the next generation prepare, and become educated, on why they should invest in your business and not start their own. Still, there are a number of useful Lessons in this book that I would want to know if I were a thirty-something year old Professional Services provider and thinking about my future.

The attributes listed above ("a" through "f") reflect the people and groups that I have spent 35 years working with first-hand (as a securities regulator, business attorney, business builder, and succession planning consultant), supported by a strong and deep team in my own Professional Services business. The "successors" in these succession plans we will explore together in the Lessons that follow are expected to purchase ownership, or equity, and invest their careers in the process. These same successors usually work in the business itself and are a key part of supporting and building the Professional Services business model.

There are dozens of books in the succession planning space written for large business organizations (with thousands to tens-of-thousands of employees, often in publicly traded companies) aimed at "organizational planning." These books focus on the proactive hiring of leaders designed to support a company's internal succession plan where the ultimate goal, and need, is to replace the CEO of the company. To be clear, these organizations and this leadership hiring, development, and replacement process are not the focus of this book. This book is about *ownership* succession of a small, closely or privately held business.

In sum, there are many Lessons provided and every founder, every entrepreneur, every business builder (even those that may fall outside of the list above and those in larger, closely held organizations of 50+ people) will benefit from the information provided regardless of business type, size, age, ownership, and value. But my intended audience is the people that I know.

PART FOUR OF THE INTRODUCTION - THE ORGANIZATION OF THIS BOOK.

Rather than presenting long and winding chapters (as I've been known to do!), the format of this book uses concise, focused Lessons, presented to you just as I have taught them to others over the years. The Lessons are certainly intended to be read sequentially, from start to finish, but may also be read individually, especially if you have already completed or figured out certain processes on your own and need to read or reread individual Lessons that you are particularly interested in.

In Lesson No. 1, I will introduce you to the unique terminology of the succession planning process and I'll help you understand some alternative pathways, including exit plans, continuity plans, and later, even the role of synthetic equity. You will have the opportunity to learn about building a special business model and, one day in the future, walking away, satisfied with the results on your own terms. Regardless of how and when you might leave the business, you've started or significantly contributed to, the intent should be that you control the process, leave your staff and clients in a better position than you found them, and monetize your investment in your own business—likely the single most valuable asset you own.

If you need additional information or have questions, please visit my website at:

www.DavidGrauSr.com

There is no cost to use this website or to email your questions, to read the blog posts or to listen to the podcasts. I welcome your continued involvement and interest. I anticipate posting additional Lessons through this channel as needed, even adding diagrams and illustrations to supplement this book, creating a dynamic reading experience. Your questions and critiques will help me, help you, better understand the complexities and the myriad possibilities afforded by this subject matter, across a wide variety of Professional Service venues. Please stop by and say hello.

You can even set up a free 30 minute one-on-one appointment to confidentially talk about your specific situation and see if a succession plan makes sense given your circumstances. If it does, I can be a guide and try to connect you with professionals who can help you with the math and finer details of your plan, if you ask. To be certain, this book and its accompanying website are all about learning and exploring. Subscribe on line at no cost using only your name and email address, confidentially of course. You will also be notified when the second book in this series is available for your next generation ownership prospects and you can enjoy some previews of the Lessons in the new companion book.

Finally, you will notice that many times in the Lessons below, I use the term "we" or "our" when providing my thoughts or guidance. I am the sole author of this book, but I did not grow up on an island. Almost everything I've learned or experienced in life and business involved others, many others, whether they knew they were sharing important and memorable lessons with me or not. I cannot individually take credit for all the wisdom out there in my small corner of the world.

And with that, *we* thank you for reading! Let's get started, shall we?

NOTATE BENE

1. Throughout this book, we will use corporate terminology, such as shares of stock, shareholders, Bylaws, Directors, Officers, and the like, to clarify and simplify important concepts without diverting from the main lessons. Limited Liability Companies actually use different terms than a Corporation, such as units of ownership, Members, and Managers, an Operating Agreement, a Members Agreement, etc. If there is a material difference from one entity structure to another other than terminology, I will tell you. Otherwise, I will focus on the concepts important to the succession planning process without immersing you in the various entity structuring terms and nuances. In the end, your final set of documents should use the terms appropriate to the entity you choose.

2. References to owners receiving *compensation for their work, being on the payroll, being employed, receiving a paycheck*, or a *Guaranteed Payment to Partner (GPP)* are to be loosely applied because it depends on the final entity structure or structures and it is certainly more than just semantics.

3. Capitalized terms used in the printed version of this book, from this point on, like Succession Planning, Successor Team, Professional Services, Residual Equity, and Exit Planning, once introduced, will reflect the definition and usage provided in the Lessons and captured in the Glossary at the end of this book for easy and quick reference.

4.   Audiobooks and eBooks travel exceptionally well, and this book will be published and available globally. While this book relies on the use of United States-based business entities, tax laws, and securities regulations, its core concepts should benefit any aspiring Professional Services owner. That said, and regardless of where you are located, you will need the help of local and professional legal/tax counsel before implementing any of the strategies in this book.

LESSON NO. 1: UNDERSTANDING THE TERMINOLOGY

(If you have not read the preceding *About the Author* and the *Four-Part Introduction,* as well as the *Important Notes* immediately preceding this Lesson, it would be a good idea to do so. There is a lot of useful information above that will make your journey through this and the following Lessons easier to understand and benefit from.)

The best way to help you understand what a succession plan is, and is not, is to get specific and to put the term into a proper context. The operative and separate terms that we will define and begin to explore in this Lesson and apply in subsequent Lessons are these:

(a) Succession Plan

(b) Exit Plan

(c) Continuity Plan

(d) Disaster Plan

To a legal, tax and regulatory professional, these are all different and important plans a Professional Services owner should consider and possibly implement. These plans are your basic pathways going forward and lest you confuse one for the other, we will explicitly define them for you. These are not generic, one-size-fits-all terms. In fact, they all have a place in your business world, just like tools in a toolbox. And before making any final decisions on your plan or plans for your own business, you need to know what you want, what you need, and what each plan can help you accomplish.

You may also notice that this Lesson begins to integrate the terms "book," "practice" and "business" as separate and distinguishable levels of ownership. Specific definitions for these terms are provided in the next Lesson because it matters where you start.

A **Succession Plan** is best defined as a documented series of steps, or tranches, designed to gradually transition ownership, leadership, and revenue production responsibilities internally to the next generation of owners (i.e., more than one next generation owner in most cases), collectively referred to as a "Successor Team." Most Succession Plans include the founder's continuing assistance and presence in the day-to-day operations for 10 to 20 years or more after the Plan starts and often well beyond any traditional retirement age if that is the goal. Succession planning is a bet on you, the founder, and what you started, who you hire, and ultimately, who you trust to carry on your work. Succession planning is a process and not a singular event.

A Succession Plan is equity-based and requires use of an entity structure. The goal is sustainability, and it is best accomplished through a Plan design and structural framework that carefully coordinates the changing roles of the founder(s) and the Successor Team members over many years. In keeping with our "corporate attributes" approach, whether working with an LLC or a corporation, we will use the terms "stock," "shares," and "units" interchangeably to represent and transact equity ownership—consider them one and the same in this book.

A Succession Plan supports the evolution of the founder's roles and skill sets from entrepreneur, to shareholder, to CEO, to mentor, maybe even to that of a residual equity owner one day. This is a sophisticated planning process that typically reflects the values and needs of the founder(s)—control, flexibility, a good return on investment, a client-centered approach, and the ability to build an enduring and transferable business, perhaps even a legacy. These are timeless elements to build in to the process starting on day one or as soon thereafter as possible.

There can be no Succession Plan without the help and support of the next generation of owners, producers or service providers, and leaders. In fact, the only way for a small practice to grow into a larger and stronger business is to attract, retain and propel next generation talent—to hire great people, support, retain and reward them, and then step aside as they gain experience and gradually fulfill their new collective roles as part of the Successor Team. These cumulative long-term investments, goals and benefits distinguish a Succession Plan from all other transition plans.

To be clear, this definition and the mechanics of this process are not like replacing the CEO at a Fortune 500 company. The members of a Successor Team for a relatively small, closely held Professional Services business are almost always full-time employees, officers, and owners/investors of that business, and even licensed if your Professional Services are regulated. That makes this process, and the people who participate in it, uniquely challenging with some lucrative benefits as well as we will explain in subsequent Lessons. Participating in a Succession Plan in every type of services business is a very firsthand process.

An **Exit Plan**, in contrast, is a complete sale of a book, practice or business to either an external third-party buyer, or an internal buyer such as a key employee, or son or daughter. Regardless of who the buyer is, the transaction is completed in one step, typically through an asset-based sale and acquisition, as opposed to a Succession Plan that involves an incremental series of stock sales. Having consulted on or watched over thousands of Exit Plan transactions, successful external buyers are usually at least two to three times the size and value of the seller; internal buyers, usually key employee(s) of the business, can succeed as well but often require more financial support or consideration from the seller(s).

In that an Exit Plan transfers business assets, rather than equity or stock, it can provide significant legal and tax benefits to the buyer that often positively, and perhaps significantly, affect the value paid to the seller. Effectively, when an Exit Plan has been completed, or the transaction closed, the new owner takes over and the acquired book, practice or business is absorbed into the buyer's business, and from the seller's perspective, ceases to exist.

A **Continuity Plan** is a written contract that provides for an orderly transfer of ownership, control and responsibility in the event one of the owners suddenly leaves the business, whether by choice or through termination of employment, a partnership dispute, loss of licensure, death, or disability. Every business with two or more owners should have a Continuity Plan, or Agreement, in place.

This particular plan can also look outside of the business when there is a single owner or when the second owner does not want the obligation to step in and buy out their partner on sudden notice. These professionally drafted agreements must anticipate a variety of triggering events and then establish rules that determine who can sell the equity and how it will be valued and paid for. Continuity Plans take the form of and are also known as a Shareholders' Agreement (as with a corporation), a Buy-Sell agreement, or an Operating Agreement that includes buy-sell provisions (for an LLC). LLCs can also separate its constitutional provisions in an Operating Agreement and its buy-sell provisions in a Members Agreement—two different documents for two different purposes.

A **Disaster Plan** is a written plan that addresses how a business will overcome one or more natural disasters (think hurricane, tornado, flood, pandemic, riots, shootings) and continue to support its clientele. These plans are sometimes voluntary and sometimes required by a regulatory body. A Disaster Plan tends to be event focused, whereas a Continuity Plan is focused on the loss of one of the owners. Various regulatory bodies confuse or overlap Continuity Plans with Disaster Plans and that is a mistake, as the issues are entirely different. If the use of a Disaster Plan is mandatory, templates are commonly provided to address the documentation process. This book will not address issues unique to a Disaster Plan, but will address Succession Plans, Exit Plans, and Continuity Plans.

Most Professional Service owners, armed with these definitions, choose a Succession Plan as their primary objective, using an Exit Plan as a secondary or fallback position. A practical Continuity Plan naturally emerges from a mature Succession Plan because the Successor Team members best serve the role as continuity partner(s) under the terms of the entity structure's buy-sell documentation. Practice owners, part of a single owner and one-generational model, often have to look for a qualified continuity partner outside of their own Practice. As such, separate documents and contractual partners are needed to address these various contingencies.

Succession Plans, when compared to Exit Plans or Continuity Plans, are unique in terms of strategy, benefits, and obligations. One of the biggest challenges in supporting a successful Plan to transition ownership is the underlying assumption that the business is going to grow—in fact, it must grow.

As businesses grow in both size and strength, they change significantly over time and leadership must make adjustments to keep up with or surpass the competition. Think about a business that grows at 10% a year in terms of gross revenue. In about fifteen years, with any kind of sustained economic tailwind, it will double in size, twice. That will be a vastly different business to operate and guide into the future and it will certainly require a higher level of talent from its bench, and a deeper bench as well.

This means that next-generation owners have an incredible opportunity to build on top of an existing Professional Services practice, enjoying the combined attributes of a steady paycheck, an established infrastructure, and a supportive team. Experience will be gained daily in this environment and the talent of the next-generation owners should flourish in time. What next generation, first-time owners universally lack is capital to invest in this opportunity, and this shortcoming affects everything from the plan length, to business value, to the founding owner's willingness to consider a Succession Plan at all. Typically, the issue comes down to one question: "Where does the money come from?" There are numerous Lessons that will help you address the answer.

Let's continue to create the necessary vocabulary so we're all speaking the same language.

LESSON NO. 2:
WHAT HAVE YOU BUILT, AND HOW HAVE YOU BUILT IT?

Respectfully, most Professional Service providers have not built and do not own a business; they own the job they do, or a practice perhaps, but not a real business as we'll define the term in this Lesson and it makes a difference, at least in terms of the starting point. As we lay out the specifics of each of these models, it should become clear that owning a job, or a book of clients, or a single-owner practice, means owning a single-generational model. As you'll learn in subsequent Lessons, the elements of a Succession Plan cannot exist in a single owner approach.

We use the synonymous terms of owning one's **Job** or owning a **Book** of clients or customer relationships to describe the base model ownership structure in the Professional Services world. A Book is best described as a single individual, often a sole proprietor, who may work from an executive suite or from home, and sometimes on a revenue-sharing basis under someone else's office lease. A Book owner, in almost all cases, has not made a significant investment in an operational structure of their own. Simply stated, the purpose of this ownership model is to generate revenue—find clients and earn a living! This is a common approach for accountants, lawyers, and financial or insurance professionals, among others. Owning a Book yields no viable Succession Plan. At career end, professionals may sell their assets, but typically their career and client base just fades away, and they refer their remaining clients to other professionals. For the sake of simplicity, we will just use the term Book when referring to this level of ownership.

By the way, lest I appear dismissive of the most common ownership structure and the starting place for so many Professional Service owners and providers, think again. Individually, Book owners can play a special role in the Succession Planning process by effectively merging into a larger, more lucrative Business, usually tax free, if the Business entity structure is set up properly in advance. We address this unique and powerful tool set in the Lessons that follow. So for the Book owners and Business owners, your two paths may be destined to cross.

The term **Practice** refers to a level of ownership that is larger and stronger than a Book. Practice owners tend to have a formal entity structure, commonly an LLC or a corporation, electing to be taxed as an S-Corporation. Practices have just one owner or shareholder. An owner of a Practice usually invests in office space through a formal lease agreement, has at least a small support staff and has the basic infrastructure (desks, computers, furniture, fixtures, etc.) to support growth, often including a Line of Credit and/or business credit or charge cards. Practices can be quite valuable, for example, in the $1,000,000 to $5,000,000 range, and may attract or operate alongside other Book owners in a coordinated fashion. A Practice is not limited to being a one-generational model—with time and a good plan, a Practice can grow into a full-fledged Business capable of supporting a long-term Succession Plan.

A **Business** is best defined for our purposes as an enterprise that is not only larger and stronger than a Practice, it is more sophisticated in its use of a professional compensation system (for employees and owners) that supports a strong bottom line on the Profit & Loss Statement. Profitability is the key to differentiating this level from the preceding two levels of ownership. Profit distributions, in turn, are used to augment the compensation system for equity owners and to recruit, retain, and reward next generation owners who invest in equity and are part of an internal Successor Team. Sustainability is the key here, and it is, or is destined to become, part of the culture of a Business, supported by a Continuity Plan or Buy-Sell Agreement among the equity partners. New hires to this level of ownership fully anticipate having the opportunity to work hard and, one day, to buy in and become an owner or equity partner of the Business.

What you've built and how you've built it is not in any way a critique of your skills or your place in the universe of Professional Service owners or providers. The various plans we explored together in our first Lesson on *Understanding the Terminology*, and how effectively you can implement such Plans, depends on where you start the journey. But be kind to yourself, as every new owner begins with their first day on the job. It's unrealistic to expect you to be as skilled as you will be in 20 years. The Plan will come together in time and with a clear direction.

The Lessons that follow assume that you have time to do some building and retooling and that you're not looking to retire tomorrow. Given time and a well-executed plan, remarkable outcomes can occur. Keep working, stay positive, and we'll get there together.

LESSON NO. 3:
THE FIVE ATTRIBUTES OF AN
EQUITY-CENTRIC BUSINESS

This Lesson starts with a philosophical paradox: *Which came first, the chicken or the egg?* And a paradox worth contemplating in the context of this book, and this particular Lesson: *What comes first, a strong business or a Succession Plan?* The process of succession planning should result in a valuable, profitable, sustainable Business; but there can be no Succession Plan without a strong, valuable, growing, underlying Business to invest in. These concepts are intricately linked, like the chicken and the egg (biologists know the answer, by the way). Let's talk about that Business.

Many entrepreneurs are often referred to as accidental millionaires. They find something that they enjoy doing or are particularly good at. They learn a lot and gain experience, make a good living and buy a nice house and…we're not talking about any of that in this Lesson! This is about a purposeful set of steps to be taken with an expected result. This is about Business ownership and Business building for the long term, designed to attract next generation investors. There is nothing accidental about this process.

The most valuable asset that most Professional Service Providers (PSPs) own is their Practice or their Business. Between the cash flow it provides, the tax benefits, and the appreciating value over time, there often is no close second. A Succession Plan empowers you to take control of this asset and make it work for you even as you get older and start to work less in the Business.

Taking control of the most valuable asset you own requires that you build the proper foundation to support the process. For starters, a Business must gradually move away from revolving around just one person's talent, drive, and personality, often that of the founder or founders, common traits of a Book or a Practice model. This seismic shift in thinking is a big part of what we call building an **Equity-Centric Business**, as opposed, perhaps, to an ego-centric business. "Equity-Centric" refers to prioritizing Equity (see our working definition of this term in the Glossary, as well as all the capitalized terms you'll read in the other Lessons) as the basis for value and success, rather than focusing on individual ownership, client services, or revenue production.

An Equity-Centric Business model serves as the concrete footings for the building of a Succession Plan. The five attributes, or elements, of such a Business are these:

1. **A shift in value** from one or more individual producers to Equity in an entity structure

2. A focus on **profitability** as the measure of business value and success

3. Building a business that, in the eyes of the next generation, is **investable**

4. A business that generates consistent top-line **growth** year-over-year

5. A multi-generational, multi-owner business that achieves **sustainability** from one generation to the next

As the succession planning process itself evolves in the wider universe of the Professional Services provider, if I could add one more attribute for the future, perhaps via honorable mention, it would be that the Business opportunity is lendable (see *Figure 1*). Investors require support from a capable money source for Equity acquisition, and a reliable banking partner plays a crucial role in this process. Sellers are more likely to be open to selling a 20% stake in their Business at Fair Market Value when they receive a check, in full, in return. To be certain, lending to a borrower purchasing a minority Equity Interest in an intangible, Professional Services Business model is not always an easy task. How to turn the tide? Work on the other five attributes! If you shift value into an entity, generate strong, consistent growth that makes it to the bottom-line of your P&L as profits, the banks will find a way to get involved and help.

Thinking this out—you cannot have a Succession Plan without these foundational elements. You could, however, set up all of these elements and still see your Succession Plan efforts fail and decide instead on an Exit Plan. Yet another possibility includes forced reliance on the terms of your Continuity Plan to bring matters to an end. Even so, I'd argue that your Business will be more valuable, more marketable, and more resilient if you can achieve even a few of these basic attributes regardless of whether the Business lasts for more than one generation. Sometimes, the best way to increase value in the eyes of an outside or third-party buyer is to walk decisively and purposefully in the other direction. Always be ready; never be desperate.

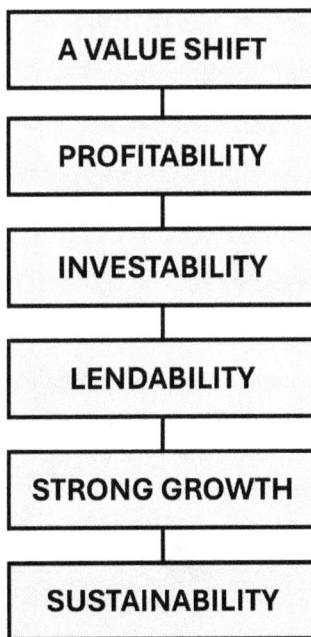

| A VALUE SHIFT |
| PROFITABILITY |
| INVESTABILITY |
| LENDABILITY |
| STRONG GROWTH |
| SUSTAINABILITY |

Figure 1

People can't work forever; a well-structured Business can indeed outlive its founder(s). As a part of this Lesson, let's explore just the first attribute of what it means to be Equity Centric. We'll cover each of the other attributes in greater detail in separate Lessons to follow. More tools in the toolbox.

Most Professional Service owners begin as forces of one, and if not as an actual sole proprietorship, then a single owner S-Corporation or LLC. From this point on, we'll refer to the preferred entity structure as "Newco, LLC", or "Newco" since it can basically adapt to any cash flow or tax structure, upon election, that an owner desires. (If you've already set up an entity, and it is something different, don't despair—the situation can almost always be resolved and/or improved as needed.) At some point early in the process, a shift must occur in which the assets of the individual entrepreneur or service provider are literally and legally transferred into Newco (see *Figure 2*), almost always some type of tax conduit which is a concept explained in greater detail in latter Lessons in this book.

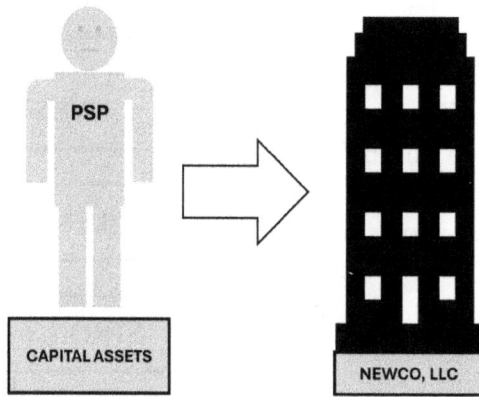

Figure2

I'd put this particular paragraph in bold type if my editor would let me because this is one of the keys to the process of setting up and building a Business. The assets of a Professional Services sole proprietorship are basically these, regardless of the profession one is engaged in: (a) the clients being served, (b) the annualized cash flow generated from serving the clients, (c) any tangible property (the physical tools of the trade or profession, whatever they may be), and (d) goodwill.

Sometimes there may be intellectual property of appraisable value as well. Collectively, we refer to these as your Capital Assets.

Using a series of legal contracts including a *Contribution Agreement,* an *Assignment & Assumption Agreement,* and a *Bill of Sale,* all rights, title and interest in the Capital Assets of the individual owner(s)/entrepreneur(s)/sole proprietor(s) are transferred into Newco in exchange for a proportional amount of equity issued by Newco. Newco then becomes the legal owner of those assets, including all future related revenue. The contributor or contributors become shareholders of Newco (see *Figure 3*). All of this typically happens privately, quietly, and without government oversight or input when setting up a new LLC, and/or having it file a tax election as either a DE (Disregarded Entity for one owner) or a Partnership (for two or more owners)—with details and further explanation in following Lessons. And at this point in the starting process, everything changes!

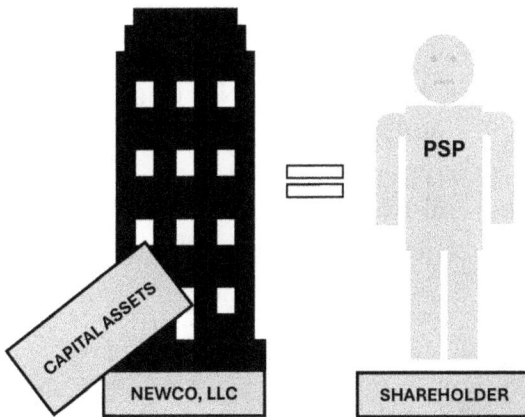

Figure 3

To further delve into this important concept, consider Newco's decision to be taxed as a DE or Partnership, with 2,000,000 authorized voting shares in a single class—as we once again apply corporate attributes to Newco as discussed in the Introduction section above. The lone contributing owner in this example, Bob, moves from individual or sole proprietor to shareholder with his conveyance of Capital Assets to Newco. The Business (with Bob as the sole shareholder, Director, and CEO) effectively trades, or exchanges, Equity for Bob's contribution of assets. Now, Bob owns 1,000,000 authorized and issued shares of voting stock and Newco owns all the Capital Assets. We'll cover the additional authorized but *unissued* shares of stock in latter Lessons but know that this is also an important part of the Business building process.

An appraiser can value the Capital Assets that Newco now holds and effectively determine a price per share. If the Business is valued at $1,500,000, for example, then each share of stock that Bob owns is objectively worth $1.50/share. This is the first step in building a Business that is more than a force of one; this is step one in implementing a Succession Plan.

It is also possible, even likely in a Professional Services model, that several affiliated individuals or Book owners, could simultaneously make such contributions into Newco upon its set-up, effectively resulting in a merger of those individual Books via a series of tax-neutral exchanges (explained further in Lesson No. 14). In such a case, Newco now owns all the contributed Capital Assets with each contributor owning Equity, proportionally, in Newco in exchange. Newco might begin operations with two, three or four partners at one time (see *Figure 4*). In most cases, this exchange process can be accomplished

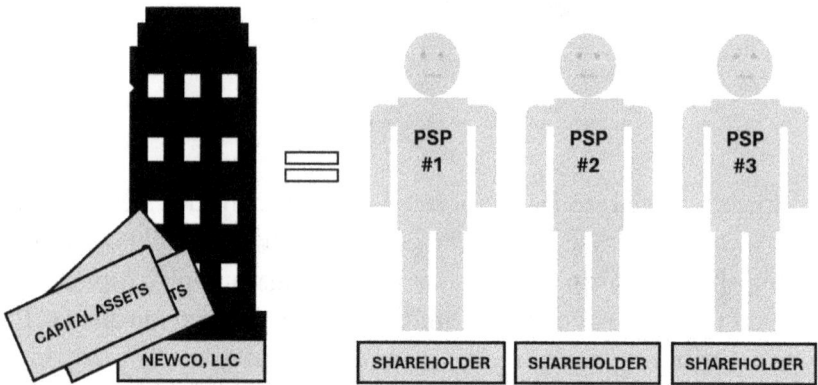

Figure 4

with no cash payments being involved, or any tax consequences to the participants, if the rules are followed.

The point is not to impress upon you that these maneuvers are easy. They are not. But these are common building blocks in the world of succession planning for PSPs and you need to know how the mechanics work to even ask the right questions of your legal and tax counsel. If you know enough to ask, an answer can usually be found. If you have surrounded yourself with younger Book owners, this is the way out, or the path forward to state it more affirmatively.

Succession planning is a powerful Business building process...and we're just getting started.

LESSON NO. 4:
DEFINING YOUR GOALS

So, how *might* your story end? Many Professional Service entrepreneurs shun the common or past retirement age thinking and plan to work for as long as possible, enjoying the Business they built and the benefits it provides. But one way or another, all individual careers end. One of the key benefits of a Succession Plan is that it can extend the length of a founder's career (if that is the goal) and, for the duration, pay that individual wages, profits, and benefits, as their stock continues to appreciate in value, with added tax savings and efficiencies, all while the owner(s) gradually reduces hours worked in the office. No other transition plan offers this complete package, or anything close to it.

I have learned over the course of several decades that goals that depend on or are attached to the talents and thoughts and skills of others far surpass goals that I set, or could set, for myself, at least in a business context. I do not mean to be judgmental, but I would like to share the thought that sometimes we, as entrepreneurs and business founders, set goals that are too easy to reach and don't challenge us to be better than we are or think we can be. Why can't we each build a business that is still serving people 50 years after our own retirements, or at least try to do that?

Whatever your goals are, take the time to write them down, and get specific. When you are finished with the first draft, set the writing aside and revisit it after some time has passed, perhaps in the quiet of a Sunday evening before a new work week begins, and add it to your list or make adjustments. Repeat this process every year and never lose sight of your written goals. Accept that your goals will change as you change. At a point early in this process, share your goals with your significant other and read them aloud, and then listen carefully to any feedback. Do not revisit this list monthly, or after a great run of success, or after a couple of bad months. The view from the peaks, or the valleys, is not accurate over the long haul, and too many course corrections make for a very bumpy ride.

A common theme that I hear from Professional Service owners is that they want to be able to monetize the value of what they have built upon retirement. This is an important goal to be sure. Cashing out or selling a Business via an Exit Plan is certainly one option and, frankly, needs to be at least a back-up plan ("Plan B" we will call it) for every Business owner. "Plan A," for most, is something more than that. In over 30 years of asking thousands of entrepreneurs this question, "How does your story end?", more than nine out of ten founding owners relate that they want to build something that outlives them, that rewards their key staff members, takes care of their clients, and allows the founder(s) the benefit of retiring at their own pace as they sell their Equity internally. That is the definition of a Succession Plan.

One of the benefits of the succession planning process is that, as a founding owner, you can craft your retirement plan to suit your needs, your age, your (changing) health, your ambitions and more. Selling Equity incrementally to a team of Successors over time means that even while you retain control and enjoy the cash flow from the Business, you can also start to slow down as responsibility for Business growth is transferred gradually to the next generation of talent that is investing in your Business and using growth to pay for, and finance, their own Equity and ambitions.

Quick aside: In the context of defining your goals, selling your Practice or Business all at once to a key employee or an outside buyer is a viable option that should be carefully considered by every Professional Services owner depending on their circumstances. An Exit Plan is the right answer for some owners. Interestingly, however, the choice between an Exit Plan and a Succession Plan doesn't appear to be even close for most Professional Service owners. Earlier in my career, I was pleasantly surprised as values started to climb for the financial advisors and related professionals that I worked with. Once we built out a national marketplace for buyers and sellers to interact and fifty buyers per seller became the norm, it seemed just a matter of time until Exit Plans outnumbered Succession Plans.

But no matter how valuable their Businesses became, nine out of ten of these Professional Service owners emphatically preferred the succession planning route. Those who chose the Exit Plan route and sold their Practices to an outside buyer often related that no matter how much they sold their Businesses for, it didn't seem like enough, and/or the deal terms were insufficient. Being pushed out the door at some point shortly after the sale, perhaps along with some of the seller's former staff, also were not welcome thoughts. Succession Planning can solve these problems over time and provides more control over the outcome.

Tax efficiencies are also a common goal of Business builders and, as you'll learn in the Lessons that follow, growing, profitable Businesses using an appropriate entity structure can help owners, young and old, take home more of their money at lower tax rates. Whether you're monetizing a lifetime of work and setting yourself up for retirement or investing your after-tax dollars to buy a minority interest in the future, tax efficiencies matter and they really add up over the extended time horizons of a Succession Plan.

Control is another common goal, worthy of its own Lesson (No. 25). I often see individual Book owners touting this (total control) as the key benefit of their existing single-owner, sole proprietorship model. The counterpoint is that if anything happens to that owner, as a force of one, who do their clients and staff look to?! Other forms of control that we'll explore in a following Lesson is that, within a multi-owner

Business, the founder can be the majority shareholder (51% +), the CEO, and the Chairman of the Board, all while monetizing their Equity at a younger age. That's control of a Business in my experience. I'd add that a real Business, by definition, doesn't disintegrate if something happens to one of the owners. That should be important to your clients as well.

I can personally attest to enjoying the changing roles of a founding owner. In the early years of my own Business, I did everything from sales and marketing, to IT and Human Resources, to customer service, to client facing delivery of products and services, to putting furniture together on the weekends! As time passed, I learned to surround myself with capable staff members and other professionals who were better, sometimes much better, at some things than I was. And then, one day, fellow owners came into the picture. In following this simple logic pathway, you can move from the sole owner into a more traditional CEO role, and beyond that, into the role of mentor and elder statesperson (that will sound better when you are in your 60s or 70s!). There is a role for everyone and for people of all ages and skills in a Business as its succession planning process unfolds. Keep this in mind as you lay out your own goals for the future. Change can be exciting.

The point is this. When defining your goals, don't consider this process as *succession planning or bust*. If you start to work on the structural aspects of your own Succession Plan early in your career, it will help you build a stronger, more durable, more valuable Business. At or nearer to your career end, things may very well look different, your needs and goals may have changed, and selling to an outside buyer just might make more sense. As you consider your goals earlier in your career, you don't have anything to lose by building a stronger, profitable, and more valuable Business in the meantime. In fact, you're likely to improve and increase your Business's value and, in the end, have more options to choose from.

LESSON NO. 5:
DEVELOPING YOUR
SUCCESSOR TEAM

A Succession Plan involves multiple owners and multiple generations of ownership who work together to build a valuable, growing, sustainable Business. The basic formula to support this process is **G1 + G2 + G3** (see *Figure 5*).

We use the term "G1" to refer to the first generation of ownership, or the founder(s), and the terms "G2" and "G3" to refer to the second and third generations of ownership. Think of these terms as *guideposts* rather than set rules for each generation or age group, though the terms are useful in conveying important concepts in the succession planning process.

As we'll explain, it is not necessary to have a full generation between each level of ownership, such as with a parent and a son or daughter. It is, however, important that the average age of each level, G1 vs. G2 vs. G3, is separated by about 15 years on average, more or less, from

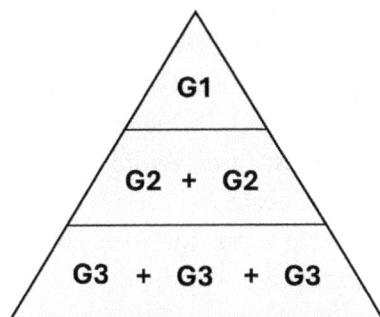

Figure 5

the other levels. The issue is that a G2 close in age to a G1 approaching retirement likely will not have sufficient time in service to fulfill a multi-tranche plan and may not be willing to incur long-term debt to fund the G1's sale of equity.

If the Succession Plan starts when G1 is 53 years of age, the basic math (including amortization schedules to support the after-tax Equity buy in process) suggests that two prospective next generation owners should be in their mid to late 30s to provide the best results (Lesson No. 21 addresses The Math of a Succession Plan). If G2(A) is 34 and G2(B) is 38, the G2s average age of 36 is used for planning and modeling purposes. This is about a 17 year average age difference compared to G1, in a simple example. Of course, there are other factors that come into play, so *the math* for each generational level of the Plan depends on your specific situation. Succession Plans are custom designed and built to address each Business's specific fact pattern and G1's goals.

The exact number of G2 owners and G3 owners over the course of a Succession Plan depends on the goals, timeframe, profitability level, growth rates and the value of the Business. This group of next generation owners (G2 + G3) is called the Successor Team. This team is usually composed of two or more younger owners who collectively (but not always equally) purchase ownership from the G1 level. In most cases, the process starts with a single key employee whose length of service with the subject Business is at least three to four years. It may be several years later that G1, working with an existing G2, adds a second member to the Successor Team, and so on. A good rule of thumb is two G2s for every owner in the G1 position, a pattern loosely repeated for the G3s who will be tasked with being the Successor Team for the G2 owners. That said, two or three G2s can buy out two G1s in most cases. Avoid having just one G2, or one person on your Successor Team, whose task is to buy out one G1; it can work, but there is no room for error and the debt load, even when spread out over time on one individual buyer, can be overwhelming.

The first member of the Successor Team is not necessarily the future

CEO and leader of the Business. A better approach is, if you have two or three next generation prospects in the first five to seven years of your Plan, start by selling each G2 the same amount of equity, such as 5%, 7.5%, or 10%. A Plan that begins with a 70%/10%/10%/10% ownership structure, for example, or even an 85%/5%/5%/5% ownership structure, allows time and circumstances to determine who is the best future leader. G1 should watch the process unfold over time and learn from the clients, the staff members, even the other owners, who the future leader of the Business should be. The temperament and skills needed to be a Business leader often differ from that of a revenue producer or willing and able investor.

Keep in mind that while the focus is on how to structure a Succession Plan over, perhaps, one to three decades, the G2 and G3 owners will also practically and legally become G1's continuity partners much sooner. In the event that G1's story ends sooner and suddenly, then the Successor Team needs to be ready and committed as a group. Dividing and conquering that significant obligation usually works best. This, plus the growing value of the Business over time, supports the logic of having more next generation owners, not less. This is also the reason the second book in this series (addressed in the Introduction section) is designed to help you more effectively recruit Book owners and G2 prospects onto your Successor Team. You will need each other and can help each other.

To this end, founding owners often struggle to find enough qualified, next generation talent to support their Plan. The concern is often expressed as "How do I find people who will work as hard and care as much about my Business as I do?" which, in fairness, is a good question that must be asked and answered. Too often, however, that question is framed to generate a nearly impossible answer in support of a self-fulfilling prophecy that G1 cannot be replaced. Back to basics—everyone can and will be replaced in a Business, using our working definition. If you are the only person who can perform the work and please the clients, then you do not own and never will own a sustainable Business.

In a growing and evolving Business, the idea is that a team of next generation owners, *each doing what they do best*, cumulatively can succeed and supplant the entrepreneurial model where the founder does all or most of the important work whether they are really good at it or not. G1 is replaced by the talents and efforts of the entire Successor Team with G1 moving from entrepreneur, to CEO, to Chairperson of the Board, to mentor, retiring when they and the Business and client base are ready. Over the decades, I've often been pleasantly surprised, and occasionally shocked, at the level of success and ingenuity these Successor Teams can generate, especially when motivated by servicing a bank loan for their Equity purchase!

In closing, define your goals and work out the details of your Succession Plan first, and then hire or integrate the next generation owners and key employees already on hand to support the Plan and the growing Business, not the other way around. The planning process, over time, is quite adaptable and can often accommodate a wide range of talents, ages, and goals if the G1 ownership level starts the process sooner than later. Doing the math (see Lesson No. 21) will help you figure out the approximate time frame and starting point.

LESSON NO. 6: TRANCHE-BY-TRANCHE

(**Note:** As a reminder, capitalized terms and acronyms like Succession Planning, Successor Team, Tranches, T1 and T2, PSPs, G1 and G2, are defined in the Glossary at the end of this book, as well as in the various Lessons. If you are not reading the Lessons sequentially, the Glossary will provide a quick and easy reference.)

A Succession Plan tends to unfold incrementally over time in a series of steps, or Tranches as we call them. Most Succession Plans have two to three Tranches which we'll explore in this Lesson using the terms T1, T2, and T3. Some Plans that start earlier or have a lot of next generation ownership talent might have four or five tranches that move around smaller amounts of Equity (but almost always in increments of 5% or more). The only rule is to work within your specific fact pattern to create a Plan that works for all involved.

Let's proceed from these basic facts. You have set up a new and appropriate entity structure which we'll call Newco, LLC, or "Newco", taxed as an S-Corporation, or a DE (Disregarded Entity) if a Partnership tax election is the goal when there is a second owner (subsequent Lessons will expound on the how and why aspects of this strategy). Following a formal contribution of all of their Capital Assets, G1 initially owns all 1,000,000 shares of issued stock (with an additional 1,000,000 shares authorized but unissued for future use) with an appraised value of $2,500,000, or $2.50/share for each share of authorized and issued stock. Value has now shifted from entrepreneur to Newco, the entity, the first attribute in an Equity-Centric Business from Lesson No. 3. Our shareholder, G1, has two G2 prospects in mind, one of whom is a long time key employee, the other being G1's son.

A good Plan design takes into account the current value of the Business, G1's estimated time to full retirement, the Business's anticipated, sustainable growth rate, profitability, and, of course, the talent level, ages, and length of service (LOS) of the G2 level prospective owners. From these basic facts, among others, the overall estimated length of the Plan is divided into a series of Tranches. Let us assume that G1 is 55 years of age and wants to work fifteen to twenty years more, slowly reducing work hours over the last half of the Plan. This fact pattern should easily accommodate a three Tranche Plan. If there is more than enough time, as in this example, each Tranche can be completely paid off before the next one starts; if the Plan needs to be condensed to fit a shorter timetable, each Tranche can overlap the previous Tranche as needed. This is part of what I often call *doing the math*.

T1 is commonly used to initiate, even validate the process and involves the first member(s) of the Successor Team acquiring a minority interest in the Business from G1. G1, once convinced that the Plan will work based on actual performance in T1 by the G2 owner(s), may choose to accelerate the Plan prior to completion of T1 and start T2 four or five years into T1, for example, even though the G2 owners may each have a ten-year amortization schedule for T1 via a conventional bank loan (or seller financing). With sufficient growth and profitability, each Tranche ideally requires about 7 to 8 years to pay off using only G2's pro rata share of profit distributions. In this respect, T2 often overlaps T1's amortization or payment schedule.

As the Plan is adjusted over time, adapting to actual growth and profitability levels, T3 might overlap T2's amortization schedule, or not. The point is that this approach allows each group of owners to adjust the speed of the Plan collectively based on their needs and abilities, and the Business's growth and success.

Conventional bank financing, if and when available to your specific Professional Services model, will often extend payment terms anywhere from five years at the low end, up to a more common ten years at the high end. A 120-month amortization schedule, however, illustrates a key point in the succession planning process. Purchasing stock, or Equity, in a growing business on an after-tax basis from one's proportional share of the profit distributions, with interest, requires time. It is a slow, methodical process. Based on G2's ability to make a down payment on the purchase price (typically a small amount, if any, in the first Tranche or two), this extended buy in approach necessitates that G1 begin the overall Succession Plan earlier than most founding owners expect.

The most common age for G1 to start a formal Succession Plan is around age 60. The best age for G1 to start their Plan is closer to fifty. More time supports a better, more manageable Plan. G1 will benefit from the extra time to put together a great Successor Team, which often results in less need to accelerate the Tranches and allows for the occasional misstep along the way (such as a G2 quitting, underperforming, or being terminated for one thing or another).

The Plan is, of course, supported by proper legal documentation including an Operating Agreement, a Buy-Sell or Members Agreement (we recommend that these be separate documents in an LLC just as they are in a corporation), Contribution Agreements, an Assignment and Assumption Agreement, a Bill of Sale, a Stock Ledger, Consent Resolutions and such. A Succession Plan should also be supported and preceded by a detailed pro forma spreadsheet modeling out the Plan for the next ten to fifteen years in detail. It is usually the pro forma spreadsheet (often professionally prepared by an experienced, credentialed Analyst) that creates "the Plan;" the legal document set supports this Plan, or at least the first Tranche of the Plan.

The point to be made here is that T2 and T3 are not formal contracts, or obligations, on G1 or the G2 owners ahead of time; in other words, G2 owners are not obligated to buy a certain amount of stock at some designated point in the future at an unknown price in an unknown economy. The spreadsheet work lays out the framework for all the Tranches and then serves as a guide to the buyers and sellers, or G1's and G2's, over the coming years. The spreadsheet model of the Plan is adapted to the realities of the Business. In a later Lesson, we'll add in the concept of being good stewards of ownership (Lesson No. 23). Stewardship rules, if and when implemented, can create an impetus for G1 to sell or at least make their Equity available for purchase at certain set times in the future. Absent this approach, after T1, the only legal obligations to buy or sell Equity occur upon a triggering event under the Business's Continuity Plan (i.e., the Buy-Sell Agreement).

Here is an example of how a typical Succession Plan might proceed, Tranche-by-Tranche, as we continue our discussion from earlier in this Lesson. In the first Tranche, or T1, depending on G1's age and retirement plans and the growth rate of the Business, G1 sells 10% (100,000 shares) of their 1,000,000 shares of equity to G2(A), and 10% (100,000 shares) to G2(B), G1's son, with a current Business valuation of $2,500,000. G2(A) and G2(B), if feasible, each obtain a conventional bank loan to finance the transaction with seller financing as an alternative (see *Figure 6*). This approach of selling a significant but minority interest in T1 is used to help address the issues of an increasing stock price over time, after-tax costs, financing ability, and, frankly, to assess G2(A)'s and G2(B)'s readiness to be significant owners and their willingness to take on and service the debt. At Fair Market Value, the buy in cost will be $250,000 for each owner—a good, meaningful and reasonable start to a Plan (Lesson No. 42 covers the possible application of a Minority Discount).

This is a significant investment, and it is meant to make the G2 owners think about it, and then fully commit or not. A G2 or G3 prospective owner who says, "Thank you, but no." is not nec-

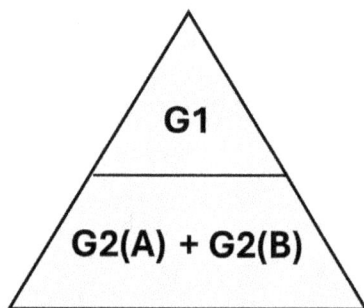

Figure 6

essarily bad news. At the G1 level, you need to know, and the sooner the better. The risk of small business ownership is not for everyone. It is important to note that when the Successor Team includes a family member, the sale price of the Equity, per share, should be the same for all buyers, with each Tranche requiring a formal valuation of the Business just prior to the transaction.

If we assume that both G2's say "Yes" to the opportunity and the obligations, the resulting ownership structure is now 80%/10%/10%, G1/G2(A)/G2(B) respectively. At this point, with the Successor Team owning 20% (and about $500,000 in value) cumulatively, G1 starts to have the makings of a reliable Continuity Plan with their internal team, though a couple of years of solid Business growth, profitability, and on-time payments by the G2s will certainly help to solidify that part of the Plan—again, you need to know. These are but a handful of the possibilities available as the Business grows, and the Plan unfolds. In the thousands of spreadsheet models for a Succession Plan we have prepared for Professional Service owners, I have never seen two exactly the same.

In this first Tranche, G1 starts to de-risk their position, realizing $500,000 at long-term capital gains rates while retaining a majority ownership level, a seat on the Board of Directors (covered in Lesson No. 24), maintaining the role of President and/or CEO. Once a quarter in the years to come, the entire ownership team should sit down and have a partner's only meeting about the Business and about the future. The pro forma spreadsheet briefly outlined above needs to be updated once a year (usually in the first quarter of each new year) as to growth rates, profitability, and compensation levels. The next Tranche, perhaps just over the horizon or perhaps not, needs to be part of the discussion. What are the plans? What has been learned from T1? What should the team do differently in T2, and maybe T3? Who else will the Successor Team need in the years to come given current growth rates?

Every Succession Plan is designed to evolve and unfold in real time, Tranche-by-Tranche.

LESSON NO. 7:
THE THREE-BASKET
CASH FLOW SYSTEM

Once Newco, LLC is properly set up, or your existing entity is re-built to support your Plan (see Lesson No. 3 for starters, and Lesson Nos. 11 through 14 for more detail), and a Taxpayer or Employer Identification Number ("TIN" or "EIN") is obtained, a business bank account can be opened. From this moment onward, with all Capital Assets having been transferred into the entity, all incoming revenue generated by Newco and its owner(s) and producers will be deposited into Newco's primary checking account which, in turn, will create the first lines of Newco's Profit & Loss Statement, or P&L.

This income should then be *compartmentalized* as it flows through the P&L to more clearly illustrate the concept of profitability as needed to support a Succession Plan through the underlying Equity-Centric Business. This Lesson is about cash flow management and rethinking the process from an investor's perspective.

Start with the notion that all incoming revenue from all owners and Professional Service Providers (PSPs) flows into three different "baskets" in Newco's Equity-Centric cash flow system (and for sake of specificity, make them hand-woven, laundry room size wicker baskets—you'll need the volume, trust me!). The first basket is set aside for general overhead expenses, the second basket is reserved for owners' compensation, and the third basket is what is left over, or profits, literally the bottom-line of Newco's P&L (see *Figure 7*). The general idea is this—overhead is the cost of running the business and encompasses all expenditures except for owner salaries. Basket No. 2 is for the owner(s) total annual base salary/salaries, or more accurately, compensation for work they perform. These two baskets serve to acknowledge that everyone, including and especially the owner(s), must be paid for the work that they do. These two baskets also provide notice that not every dollar of revenue after overhead expenses from Basket No. 1 have been paid is allocated to the owner's salary as it would be in a sole proprietorship (the training grounds for most entrepreneurs).

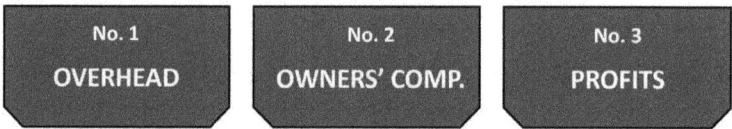

No. 1	No. 2	No. 3
OVERHEAD	OWNERS' COMP.	PROFITS

Figure 7

In fact, there are often tax advantages to be gained by isolating and limiting the amount of money paid through Basket No. 2, in deference to Basket No. 3 (we'll address the issue of "Reasonable Compensation" later in Lesson No. 13). In the end, it is Basket No. 3, profits or profitability, which is the measure of success and the primary determinate of Business value. To an investor (a term used broadly to include all owners of the Business), Basket No. 3 provides the return on each owners' investment (or "ROI"). Every small business and Professional Service venue is unique but let's start out with a rule of thumb of 25% profitability as a reasonable, near-term future goal and adjust from there, acknowledging that some Professional Services can only generate half that, and others, twice that. The profitability of a given Professional Services Business varies widely depending on factors such as location, specialty, and management efficiency. The Lessons and the logic still apply regardless of what *normal* profitability is for your specific Professional Services model.

If Newco, for example, generates $1,000,000/year in gross revenue for services rendered, then after Basket Nos. 1 and 2 are satisfied, $250,000 flows to the bottom-line of Newco's P&L and flows home, pro rata, to the owner(s) of this tax conduit or flow through entity structure. Basket No. 3, along with a paycheck for work performed from Basket No. 2, is a large part of what creates and supports the concept of a Business being investable for the Successor Team members. But to be clear, the only way to access the dollars in Basket No. 3, often in a more tax efficient manner as compared to Basket No. 2, is to take the risk of ownership and buy Equity.

Though not directly a function of the Three Basket Cash Flow System, the concept of being investable is bolstered by top-line growth (see Lesson No. 10 - *Grow, Grow, Grow!*). As long as that growth is profitable and, perhaps, scalable the Business itself should appreciate in value. Stock appreciation, along with profit distributions and a paycheck can make a monetary investment in a Professional Services Business a unique and rewarding proposition. To be clear, making your Business investable is different from making it saleable.

One of the primary goals of using this Three-Basket Cash Flow System is to help newer, younger owners learn to *think like an owner*. Building a valuable Business means everyone needs to keep an eye on the general overhead of the Business. Given that the next generation owners who buy equity will need to use much of their future profit distribution checks from Basket No. 3 to pay for their investment, growing the top-line of the Business while limiting the overhead expenses and owners' compensation leads to greater value and a shorter debt service period. (Of course, it also supports a higher Business valuation and share price as well, putting G1 in a strong selling position over time.) Effectively, the Successor Team members are motivated to use "smart and efficient growth" to address their debt service obligations, and they are expected to do just that if given the opportunity.

There is no set formula that works for every Professional Services Business but assume that in our example above, Basket Nos. 1 and 2 cannot collectively exceed 75%, leaving 25% to the bottom line, or Basket No. 3. If the necessary overhead to run your Business is around 50% of annual gross revenue, then Basket No. 2 should be limited to 25% in order to obtain the desired level of profitability at 25%, referred to as a 50/25/25 cash flow system. Alternatively, if the goal is 30% profitability and the overhead in Basket No. 1 is coming in around 40% T-12 (trailing twelve months), then you can allocate up to 30% to owner's compensation, or a 40/30/30 cash flow system.

For those Professional Service owners whose venue has much higher overhead that, in turn, reduces profitability to the 10% to 15% range, please keep reading. Doctors, dentists, veterinarians, lawyers, just to list a few such learned professionals, are expensive to hire and retain, but the Lessons on how to balance cash flows more effectively and how to use Equity to hold expenses and salaries down in favor of more tax efficient rewards (stock appreciation and profit distributions) are still very much worth considering. At the very least, bolstering profitability by even a couple percentage points over your competitors could change the value of your Business significantly whether you build it for Succession or sell it as part of an Exit Plan.

Every Business ownership team must find what works best for their Professional Services model and its geographical setting (which impacts the cost of doing business). The answers as to the proper cash flow system for any given Business often come from the pro forma spreadsheet modeling process. Of course, anything and everything works in this system where there is just one owner; modeling for two or three owners is a revelation!

We will further explore different strategies, tax efficiencies, and *the math* for supporting a Succession Plan in the Lessons that follow using this Three-Basket Cash Flow System, including a unique merger strategy involving Book owners. This cash flow system we have begun to explore in this Lesson is a simple concept that supports sophisticated planning strategies.

Your toolbox may well be a hand-woven wicker basket. Who would have thought?!

LESSON NO. 8:
MAXIMIZING PROFITABILITY

The second characteristic of a Business that focuses on Equity (from Lesson No. 3) is profitability.

From an appraiser's point of view, the bottom-line of an Equity-Centric Business's Profit & Loss Statement is the starting point for building a valuable Business. Annual gross revenue is often the primary measurement tool for success relied on by sole proprietorships (filing one or more Schedule C's on their tax returns), including most Book and Practice owners, while profits are the primary measurement tool for Business owners. Profits, or what's left after all expenses and at least reasonable compensation to the owner(s) has been paid, is what investors are interested in because profits support growing share value and serve as the answer to the question, "Where does the money come from for a G2 to buy in?". Profits are also one of the key factors that a next generation (G2 and/or G3) investor's bank looks to when considering a conventional or SBA loan to support such an investment—this is the developing attribute of being lendable.

Basket No. 3 defines success, but smart owners focus on managing Baskets Nos. 1 and 2 to achieve the necessary levels of profitability (see *Figure 8*).

Overhead expenses, to a large degree, are the most difficult category to significantly reduce or change, though this cash flow category certainly warrants a firm hand at all times. Most Practices, as they make the turn towards a Business, start with lower profitability as compared to what they'll have in years to come or what a well-run competitor Business might have. A lower profitability picture might appear as 50%/40%/10%, applying our Three-Basket Cash Flow System. Again, I'll concede that almost everything works as to Basket No. 2 with an ownership team limited to the founder or founders since their base wages are augmented by the profits flowing through Basket No. 3, at least in the tax conduit models utilized in these Lessons. The G1 ownership level can simply decrease the amount of cash in Basket No. 2 and effectively increase the amount of cash in Basket No. 3, within reason as it all flows through to the owners pro rata.

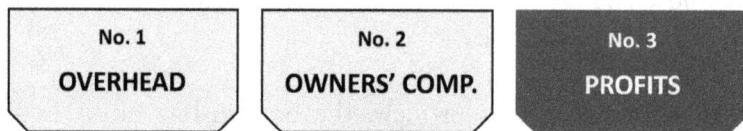

No. 1	No. 2	No. 3
OVERHEAD	OWNERS' COMP.	PROFITS

Figure 8

The challenge and the opportunity to fix your cash flow model for long-term success and profitability comes when new, next generation investors join the ownership team. A simple and firm rule to understand is that new owners won't buy equity, shoulder a ten-year amortization schedule, *and take a pay cut.* Whatever wages they have enjoyed recently as employees or Book owners, including any annual bonus, will translate into their full wages as an owner more times than not. As such, G2's entrance into the equation tends to reset all the cash flow numbers, starting with Basket No. 2, and it usually turns out to be a good thing over time. Let's examine that premise in more depth.

Consider what happens when G2(A), a key employee, acquires Equity in a given Business. G2(A) stops being an expense (no disrespect intended) and shifts over to Basket No. 2 with the other G1(s)—their wages come out of this second, controllable cash flow Basket. At this point, however, there are more changes than might be immediately apparent. Basket No. 2 wages, for example, do not need to change every year thereafter. Owners have more ways, and better ways, of being paid and building wealth than just wages plus a bonus, all at ordinary income tax rates.

Applying a stabilizing strategy to Basket No. 2 wages for all owners (see Lesson No. 35, *The Plateau Level Compensation Strategy*) has the effect of freezing owners' compensation for three or four years at a time. This strategy is part of helping new, younger investors learn to think like owners and focus on growing the Business, watching general overhead expenses, and increasing profits.

The reason that you might consider this approach and freeze all the owners' compensation levels (owners can and should be paid different salaries based on their tenure, roles, and other factors) is because of the combined effects of profit distributions in a growing, efficient Business. As the Business continues to grow on the shoulders of more owners, with everyone watching general overhead in Basket No. 1, and with Basket No. 2 stabilized, where do the new growth dollars go? In the years ahead, a portion of the new growth dollars will be allocated to Basket No. 1, but not all of them. By directing little to no new growth funds into Basket No. 2, profitability will greatly improve as most of the money goes straight to the P&L's bottom line.

Nothing brings these concepts home like a forward-looking pro forma spreadsheet. You have to do the math to figure out the right numbers for all the parties, the necessary and attainable growth rates, and the sacrifice in annual salary increases that everyone is willing to make in order to maximize profitability, and Business value. In an 80/10/10 ownership structure where G1 gets 80% of the profits, this approach may not work for the G2 owners. In a more equal 40/30/30 ownership structure, this approach works easily almost every time. In sum, this approach helps to reset the cash flow system and enables a Business *to* grow through the profitability problem and strengthen the bottom-line over time. But the story does not end there. It gets better!

As you will learn in the entity structuring Lessons (Nos. 11, 12, and 13), many small businesses and Professional Service owners utilize an S-Corporation structure as its business model (or in its business model) that can reduce taxes on the dollars flowing through Basket No. 3, assuming at least reasonable compensation is paid through Basket No. 2. This leads to a natural tendency with equal levels of ownership to *overweight* Basket No. 3 as the Business continues to grow and settles the allocations as to the first two cash flow Baskets. I've observed that a number of highly valuable Professional Service models have successfully implemented cash flow systems such as 30/30/40, or sometimes even 30/20/50, over time.

If your profession lies in a higher overhead model and you start this process at 50/40/10, imagine the impact by shifting two key employees into ownership through a purchase or tax-neutral exchange and steadily moving towards a 40/40/20 cash flow system. Doubling the level of profitability will significantly impact the value of the Business and make it more investable and lendable.

This restructured cash flow system encourages the formation of a team of colleagues who rely on each other to service a collective client base, building value in a single enterprise designed to last for generations to come. When a key employee, son or daughter, weigh the opportunity to purchase Equity in the Business where they work, they need to see several years of formal Profit & Loss Statements and observe the historical overhead of the business, how much the owners have been and are currently paid for the work that they do, and the amount of profit dollars *actually distributed* to the owners over that time. Stock appreciation matters as well, but it does not provide annual cash flow as a benefit. This describes the process of due diligence as conducted by an investor. Balancing these cash flow categories and maximizing profitability is what makes a Business valuable, investable, lendable, and sustainable. The point is that you cannot do this on the eve of pitching the opportunity to one or more next generation investors.

To get to the right answer(s) for your Business, you have to do the math, and, ironically, the route to profitability starts with Basket No. 2, ownership compensation. Let's keep building on this concept.

LESSON NO. 9:
RETHINKING OWNERSHIP
COMPENSATION IN LIGHT
OF SHAREHOLDER VALUE

It is worth noting that we've been working with the Three-Basket Cash Flow System in the last two Lessons and we'll continue to apply it here for even greater context. Basket No. 2 in this cash flow system, as you may have guessed by now, is the variable. Overhead expenses can be adjusted/reduced over time by a few percentage points, but for the most part it costs what it costs to run a growing Business. As such, maximizing Business profit levels needs to be a primary goal for every Business owner because it is the key to determining business value. Business value, in turn, is the single, largest most valuable asset most Equity owners will have. Basket No. 2 sits in the middle and is what makes this new cash flow system all come together (see *Figure 9*).

Practically, I have observed and personally found it to be advantageous

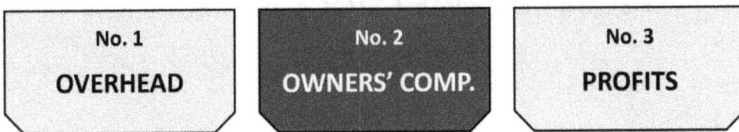

No. 1	No. 2	No. 3
OVERHEAD	OWNERS' COMP.	PROFITS

Figure 9

to set aside enough money in Basket No. 2 (owners' compensation) to pay all of my personal bills (mortgage, groceries, cars, insurance, savings, wine cellar, etc.) except for my city, county, State, and federal level taxes. Maxing out your Social Security contributions may also be a consideration if you're so inclined. Yes, a lot of this is entrepreneurial level thinking (my training ground as well!) but let's take this step-by-step for now.

I spent quality time as a sole proprietor before building a valuable, profitable, sustainable Business and subsequently had to rethink how owners' compensation should work for a group owners. As a sole prop or a single owner, I worked through some especially strong economic headwinds along the way including the Great Recession. I also lived in a city, county and state with very high income taxes. When you're at the helm of a very fast growing small business and the economy forces a sudden stop or a slowdown, even after making all your quarterly estimated payments based on the prior year's income—well, you learn to rethink cash flows a bit. It's called survival! When you experience fast growth, it's common to owe taxes on tax day, which can vary from a small to a significant sum. That's a good problem if you're in total control of the cash flow system, but your G2's won't be, for a long time to come.

Moving this discussion to a higher level and building on the last Lesson, it is important to consider that *total take home pay*, we'll call it, to an Equity owner in a Business, dollar-wise, is about more than just Basket No. 2—a lot more. With that, let's introduce the concept of Shareholder Value. This is *what's in it for you* as a founding owner (G1) or, in the future, as a member of the Successor Team (G2/G3):

FOR G1 OWNERS: WAGES + PROFIT DISTRIBUTIONS + EQUITY INCOME + STOCK APPRECIATION

FOR G2/G3 OWNERS: WAGES + PROFIT DISTRIBUTIONS (- DEBT SERVICE) + STOCK APPRECIATION

Shareholder Value, as expressed on an individual basis over a ten-year forecast on a pro forma spreadsheet in a growing Business, is the reason the next generation of talent will invest (or not) in what you've started and continue to build. This package of benefits cannot be touched or simulated (using Synthetic Equity for instance) for key employees who are not owners, or who do not take the risk of purchasing equity.

As a G1 owner, the mechanics of the process work this way in most cases: monthly wages for the work you do at ordinary income tax rates + quarterly profit distribution checks for the ownership you hold at slightly less than ordinary income tax rates via an S-Corporation structure + equity income at long-term capital gains (LTCG) tax rates minus any basis you might have as stock is incrementally sold at Fair Market Value (FMV) + stock appreciation which grows tax free until one day you sell it at LTCG rates. The strategy is pretty simple—if you can take home the same amount of money over time at lower tax rates, why not do that? An Equity-Centric Business provides greater tax efficiencies even as it supports a long-term Succession Plan.

Given these concepts, I've seen Professional Service Business owners construct, over several years, a 40/10/50 cash flow model. As long as your CPA/EA will sign off on Basket No. 2 meeting reasonable compensation requirements in an S-Corporation or LLC/S-Corporation tax setting, it might make sense. For those Professional Service owners in a higher overhead model, again, even the ability to double the level of profitability will make a significant difference in a ten-year cash flow projection, or at least it will for your investors!

> **Quick aside:** Understand that even if you can increase the amount of money allocated to and paid out from Basket No. 3, it does not automatically increase the value of your Business beyond a certain point. Appraisers, lenders, and investors will re-evaluate your cash flow numbers in light of industry norms, a function referred to as normalizing the cash flow. Normalizing a Business's cash flow to re-allocate *more appropriately* to the other two Baskets, in hindsight, is done to make sure the Business can actually be oper-

ated in a commercially reasonable and competitive manner. One owner, for instance, might take a bare minimum salary to pass the IRC reasonableness requirement and work 75 hours a week to keep the overhead low as well, proudly operating a 30/10/60 cash flow system. Such efforts will usually not be rewarded in full by an investor, appraiser, or lender. Still, if you can increase tax efficiencies through an S-Corporation or an LLC/S-Corporation, there might be a good argument for doing so anyway.

In most cases, profitability or EBITDA (earnings before interest, taxes, depreciation and amortization), is capped at a high of around 50%, depending on the circumstances and the type of Professional Services venue you work in. If you're a veterinarian and struggle to achieve 10% profitability, suddenly doubling Basket No. 3 by halving Bucket No. 2 may well be met with the same normalizing approach, at least to some extent. The takeaway here is that your Three-Basket Cash Flow System can work any way you'd like when you're the only person it has to serve; once you have investors, things will change to benefit the entire group of owners.

G1 is wise to consider these cash flow baskets, or at least the conceptual framework, from the vantage point of next generation owners. What's in it for the G2 or G3 owners? Simply go back to the Shareholder Value formula above in this Lesson for the complete answer. As an investor with debt to service from the equity purchase, profit distributions need to be sufficient to pay off the debt entirely on an after-tax, plus interest basis in about 7 to 8 years using most, but not all, of the buyer's pro rata profit dollars. If the buyer's bank will lend on a ten-year term, this leaves plenty of room to spare in most instances (with any surplus profit dollars augmenting the G2/G3 buyer's wages). To be clear, G2 will need most, but not all of their Basket No. 3 dollars to service the Equity buy in debt, but none of their Basket No. 2 dollars, at least on a pro forma cash flow model (banks don't really care where the money comes from as long as the debt is paid in full and on time).

The point to be made here is this. Basket no. 2 is what pays the bills at

home and it's usually spoken for. Stock appreciation or, said differently, the top-line growth rate of the business over time less overhead and
owners' compensation is what really builds wealth as stock appreciates
tax-free until it is sold; it just doesn't pay any bills in the near term.
Attracting investors, even those who already work for you, requires
that you find an appropriate and attractive balance in your cash flow
system and present the package in terms of Shareholder Value. That's
rethinking things like an owner.

LESSON NO. 10:
GROW, GROW, GROW!

The concept is relatively simple: multiple generations of motivated owners working together are capable of generating higher revenue growth over a longer period than a single, experienced but aging founder. It is the execution that is sometimes complex!

Top-line growth rates work well as a measure of growth from one year to the next for small businesses and Professional Service owners. Gross revenue numbers are typically available to all founders even from their days as sole proprietorships and tracking such growth over increments of three to five years is informative to an owner (and investor). If, for example, a Business grows in terms of top-line gross revenue from $1,000,000 to $2,000,000 over a five-year period, that will equate to a CAGR (Compound Annual Growth Rate) of 14.9%/year. Profits are still the ultimate measure of value and success, but they aren't the only measurement tool an owner should rely on.

The calculation process of a CAGR requires three inputs: (1) the beginning value, (2) the ending value, and (3) the time period. A CAGR takes into account the effect of compounding which means that the growth builds upon itself. The CAGR formula is equal to (Ending Value/Beginning Value) ^ (1/No. of Periods)-1, though you may find it easier, as I did, to just use one of the free on-line calculators available to measure your CAGR over any number of years you choose.

Let's talk about why it matters. I met a gentleman midway through my career who owned a Professional Services Business in the field of wealth management and insurance. He led a successful team for over 40 years and, when he sold the last of his equity to his three G2's at age 75 and retired (with an appraised value just north of $25 million), he told me his simple philosophy: "If a small business doesn't grow by at least 15% a year, topline, it's dying." Take that for what it's worth. As a business owner, it became my North Star.

Growth is particularly important in the Succession Planning process, though it does not require a 14.9% CAGR into perpetuity to make it work. Strong, steady, profitable growth is the goal and predictability matters to those who are or will be investors. A simple and effective way to approach the growth process, and to set goals for the Business, is to calculate how long it will take to double in size (especially with help from additional owner(s) and innovative ideas). The time to double in size is 70 divided by the constant annual growth rate you're targeting. For instance, consider an annual target growth rate of 10%. According to the *Rule of 70*, it will take 7 years (70/10) for the quantity to double. At an annual growth rate of 15%, your Business will double in value in just over four and a half years (70/15 ='s 4.67). This is thinking about where your Business is going. How it gets there is a different matter.

There is a common misperception by smaller Book builders and Practice owners (e.g., sub $1,000,000 in gross annual revenues) that a top-line growth rate of 10% to 15%, or more, is unsustainable as a Business grows larger. Having been there and done that, I would argue the opposite. In fact, as a Business gets larger it can and should develop a stronger and deeper bench of talent. It has the ability, for example, to invest specifically in the marketing and sales functions (and perhaps not tasking individual owners and PSPs to be the engine of growth through revenue production and client acquisition). As a result, with growth, the Business's leadership should have the funds to hire key staff members who actually have education, skills, and experience in the marketing of a Professional Services Business, in your specific venue. A larger Business, armed with an adequate budget and clear, specific growth, marketing, and sales goals to achieve as a coordinated group on an annual basis is arguably better positioned to consistently grow at higher levels and for longer periods of time than a smaller Book or Practice. That has been my experience over the past 30 years.

Books and Practices, as we defined the terms in Lesson No. 2, depend on a single individual who attempts to serve as the head of client services, marketing and sales, HR, IT and so on. At some point, such an individual will simply *run out of gas*, or *hit a ceiling*, or whatever metaphor you'd prefer. It is inevitable. The building of an Equity-Centric Business supports, even demands, a gradual shift from the force of one growth model to a complete team, assembled one person at a time, one investor at a time, one expert in their field at a time, for decades. Theoretically, well run, growing Businesses are immortal... and that is part of why they're investable. Practically, we'll just focus on a generation or two at a time and call it good.

In revisiting a previous Lesson, always consider your growing Business in terms of its future trajectory. A 10% CAGR means that over the course of 15 to 20 years, a common succession planning timetable, your business will change significantly. Your Business will double in size twice over at this growth rate, even given obstacles that might reduce growth to zero or negative for a year or two along the way. At the other end of this growth tunnel, your Business may well have different clients with diverse needs, served by more staff members who need increased expertise to meet those needs. Ask yourself the questions, "What will my business need when it is 2X in size? 4X in size?!" and plan accordingly. Build for that Business! Do you have the right people? What other talent sets will that new Business need to have to keep growing, satisfying, and attracting new clientele?

And know that slower growth can still support a Succession Plan, though it will have an effect on value and how investable the opportunity is perceived to be.

In the end, growth is what next generation owners who make an

Equity investment depend on to support their purchase decision and to service their debt. Top-line growth channeled through an efficient cash flow system into bottom line profitability increases the Equity value over time, perhaps doubling that value several times over the course of a generation. To make it all work, *the top line revenues have to grow* and the responsibility for such growth must be shared by all owners, young and old, and transfer at some point from the G1 level to the Successor Team (G2s and G3s) members.

The best way to complete such a significant transfer is to build the proper systems and procedures together. Hire the talent to market and sell your Professional Services. It is an investment that must be made at some point; an investment that will allow leaders to lead, service providers to provide services, marketers to market, and sales people to sell. However it happens, one of the essential functions in building a valuable, sustainable, multi-generational business is this: Grow, Grow, Grow!

LESSON NO. 11:
ENTITY STRUCTURING BASICS

These entity structuring Lessons (Nos. 11 through 14) apply even if you have already set up an entity on your own. A Succession Plan relies on a unique structure of cash flow modeling, tax efficiencies, and a Tax-Conduit, among other things. The good news is that most existing entities can be readily adapted or amended to work with this process.

An entity structure is akin to the concrete footings and support or stem walls poured when building a new home—one of the very first steps in the building process. The footings and concrete walls, mostly below ground level, provide rigidity and every part of the house is in one way or another attached to or supported by this solid foundation built to last for generations. Generally, when the home is complete and move-in ready, these support elements are hidden from sight and are barely noticed, but there is no house without this critical functional part of the whole.

In this first of four entity structuring Lessons, we will start with important basics that you need to know and progress to the specific details and options.

> **Quick aside:** Here is some good general advice from a former securities regulator, attorney, and Professional Services Business builder: when you hit $1.0M ($1 million) in gross annual rev-

enue, no one should remain a sole proprietorship! It's time to formalize your operations and add in some tax efficiencies, limit your liability, formally separate your personal and business assets. This step will also provide you with more options for the future.

Sometimes, a simple S-Corporation is all that is needed, though larger, sustainable Professional Service Businesses sometimes require a more sophisticated and flexible structure that is built using a Limited Liability Company (LLC). As this and the following Lessons will explain, there are usually two or three good, workable entity choices in most cases, in most states, and for most professions. My goal in this book is to help you figure out which one may be best for your needs or, if you already have an entity, if you have the right one. Final choices will need to be verified by local tax and legal counsel, but these Lessons should help you understand the finer points of that discussion and, at the very least, what questions you should be asking.

Remember that a Succession Plan starts with a transfer of assets and value from individual producers or service providers into the entity. The entity then issues Equity as shares of stock, or units, in exchange, to each contributing owner. The owners, especially the founders in our explorations, can then sell a portion of their Equity to next generation owners or prospective investors. These are the basic workings of a Succession Plan. Stock can be transferred, for value, in increments as small as one share, but more commonly at 50,000 shares to 200,000 shares per Tranche (assuming that, in our examples, 1,000,000 total shares of stock are authorized and issued, or outstanding). This is why you need an entity.

Some entities such as C-Corporations and LLC's taxed as Partnerships can issue more than one class of stock, but in almost every case, Professional Service Businesses setting up a Succession Plan only need one class of Equity. In my experience, most Professional Service Business owners benefit from a Tax-Conduit or flow-through structure that can provide a tax efficient return on an owners' investment. Professional Service Businesses capable of producing an elevated level of profitability and flowing these profits pro rata into the hands of its founder(s) and next generation owners help to address many of the issues for those who are considering the investment risk of a minority ownership position. The entity also serves to frame cash flows and applicable tax rates for the Business and its shareholders. For all these reasons and more, unless a Professional Services Business intends to raise capital from venture capitalists or outside investors, a C-Corporation may be eliminated from consideration for most Professional Service Businesses seeking to set up a Succession Plan.

It is possible, of course, that you may currently be operating as a C-Corporation because no one thought to make the Subchapter S election or because a choice was made to accumulate assets within the corporation rather than flowing profit to its owners. A C-Corporation can change to a S-Corporation, but to avoid recapture tax there is an exclusion period. If you are considering switching from a C- to an S-Corporation, you should plan ahead after speaking to your tax advisor.

Additional benefits of setting up an appropriate entity include:

- A clear and effective governance structure supported by officers, directors, shareholders, and employees
- The ability to "onboard" or merge smaller Book owners into the entity via a tax neutral exchange process (covered in Lesson No. 14)
- Limited liability for the equity owners in certain situations

Corporations and LLCs both offer limited liability benefits. Limited liability is always good for an owner, but it often doesn't work quite the same for a Professional Services owner in a regulated business. Generally, the owners of a properly structured and maintained entity are not personally liable for business debts or lawsuits. Professional Service owners may, however, remain liable for their own negligence and for any obligations for which they've signed a personal guarantee. The combination of an entity that offers limited liability plus Errors & Omissions (E&O) insurance usually provide the necessary protection.

In terms of supporting a Succession Plan, the underlying entity structure options for most Professional Service Businesses come down to these choices in most states, with each choice explained in more detail in the following three Lessons:

(a) An LLC that elects to be taxed as either a Partnership or as an S-Corporation

(b) A corporation making an S-Corporation tax election

(c) A hybrid model that utilizes an LLC/Partnership as the main, Equity-Centric Business (into which all revenue is deposited) with a supporting satellite Member S-Corporation or LLC/S-Corporation for each owner

A fourth choice, depending on the state you're located in and the type of Professional Service being offered, is a PC (Professional Corporation), or a PLLC (a Professional Limited Liability Company). Most states limit the type of people who may create a Professional Corporation and, generally, these include accountants, engineers, physicians and other healthcare professionals, lawyers, and veterinarians. A Professional Corporation is governed by state law, and states have restrictions which may require a majority of the ownership to be in the hands of licensees or may prohibit unlicensed owners altogether. In most cases, a PC or PLLC can be used to support a Succession Plan provided the owners can meet their state's specific rules and their licensing board's regulations.

LESSON NO. 12:
ENTITY STRUCTURING
CHOICES (AN LLC)

A Limited Liability Company is considered by most attorneys and accountants to be the most flexible and fluid type of entity and this general choice tends to be favored as a result. LLC's can also be a bit complicated, in my experience, having been an owner of one for 25 years. Here's what you need to know.

An LLC comes to life when *Articles of Organization* are filed with the Secretary of State, usually in the state where the Business's primary office is located. From this point on, as long as you pay your annual renewal fee, the state will recognize your Business as an LLC or Limited Liability Company. Once the Articles have been approved, you can obtain an Employer Identification Number (EIN) through the IRS's online portal and open a bank account. That's the easy stuff. Once you have successfully filed your LLC, the founding owner or owners can then choose, as a group, to have the LLC taxed in one of the following four ways:

1. a DE, or Disregarded Entity (if there is only one owner)

2. a Partnership (if there are two or more owners)

3. a C-Corporation, or

4. an S-Corporation

This tax election process, along with the ability to subsequently change the election under certain circumstances over the coming years as your Business needs change, is why an LLC is considered to be so flexible. With a single filing, your LLC can be whatever you need it to be. There is almost no good reason not to set up an LLC as your basic structure. The nomenclature used in this book to refer to an LLC that elects to be taxed as a DE, Partnership, or S-Corporation, is simply LLC/DE, LLC/Partnership, or LLC/S-Corporation, respectively.

To be clear, you hold out to the public as an LLC, or as a Limited Liability Company, but you separately hold out to the taxing authorities (city, county, state, and federal) based on the underlying tax election, kind of a two-dimensional entity structure! For our purposes, there is virtually no difference between filing as a corporation or an LLC when electing S-Corporation tax treatment other than the flexibility to start your LLC with a different tax election initially.

> **Quick aside:** The election of tax treatment is solely made with the IRS, and then each state in which the Business operates will recognize the entity as such. If there is one owner of an LLC, it is automatically taxed as a DE unless it files an S election (Form 2553). If there are two or more owners of an LLC, it is automatically taxed as a Partnership unless it files a Form 2553. An LLC with two or more owners may file a Form 8832 with the IRS to declare that it intends to be taxed as a Partnership but doesn't have to.

An LLC affords its equity owners the ability to migrate between these four choices, though the best way to think about it is that one can migrate from the first choice (DE) to the fourth choice (S-Corporation) *as a one-way trip.* If you migrate over time from an LLC/DE with one owner, to an LLC/Partnership with two or more owners, and then to an LLC/C-Corporation that makes an S-Corporation election, you will probably need to retain your S-Corporation tax status from then on as there can be significant taxes/penalties to backtrack after the Business has grown substantially. There are a lots of rules and exceptions to additionally consider, but those are the basics.

Since a Succession Plan depends on a high level of profit dollars flowing to each owner pro rata through a Tax Conduit structure, the C-Corporation, as a permanent option, can be eliminated from consideration for most Professional Service owners. That said, the remaining three choices are all viable options for a Professional Services Business. Inasmuch as we will cover entities that make an S election in the next Lesson, the remainder of this Lesson, after a bit of context, will focus on an LLC that has two or more owners and elects taxation as a Partnership. This is where flexible and fluid meets sophisticated.

Starting on the ground floor, an LLC treated by the tax authorities as a DE is a one-owner entity structure—the IRS disregards the entity for tax purposes and treats the owner as a sole proprietorship, albeit one with limited liability—and fits our working definition of a Practice covered in an earlier Lesson. Initially, and often until next generation owners join the Business, most LLC's start out as a DE, though the next step with two or more owners is what really matters in a growing Business with a Succession Plan. Once there is a second owner, the tax election defaults from a DE to that of a Partnership, although the addition of the new owner is the time to make a considered election of your preferred tax classification, which at this writing is accomplished by filing form 8832.

An LLC taxed as a Partnership is a unique entity choice affording a wide range of flexibility and adaptability to a growing, changing Business, especially over several generations and perhaps in a regulated profession. For example, an LLC/Partnership can accommodate multiple classes of equity should you or the next generation ever need that option, and it can utilize virtually any type of Synthetic Equity plan you can imagine, subject matter covered in Lesson No. 19. Partnership law also allows owners to allocate profits and losses based upon criteria other than ownership percentage, and it may eliminate or reduce state-mandated requirements imposed on corporations, such as annual meetings and minutes.

An LLC/Partnership offers a distinct advantage over all the other entity structuring options in that it allows for the exchange an incoming owner's Book (cash flow, client relationships, goodwill) for equity in the LLC/Partnership in a tax-neutral manner, which permits the Business to "onboard" or merge in next generation talent. This is a powerful growth and talent acquisition/retention tool covered separately in Lesson No. 14. Onboarding talent with ownership experience and a Book to contribute, completely resets the table in the world of Succession Planning. It is something that every small business owner should consider seriously—this element is all about building with the end in mind.

So what is the bad news? There are a couple of things to know. An LLC/Partnership, unlike an LLC/S-Corporation or even a basic S-Corporation, cannot treat an owner as a W2 employee, and it cannot offer a tax savings on the payment of profit distribution dollars (from Basket No. 3). As a past owner of an LLC/Partnership, I can also attest that this is the most complicated entity structure on the planet, or at least it is on the shortlist. Partnership tax law is voluminous and written in many shades of gray. What that means is that you may require a more sophisticated accountant or CPA (and potentially, a tax attorney) who has experience providing guidance to Businesses with the same entity and tax structure you have chosen. In sum, an LLC/Partnership is powerful, flexible, and a bit complicated. I prefer the word sophisticated, but it depends on the issue you are trying to address.

LESSON NO. 13:
ENTITY STRUCTURING CHOICES
(AN S-CORPORATION)

A corporation electing to be taxed as an S-Corporation can be a smart choice for most Professional Service Practices that want to grow into an Equity-Centric Business in support of a Succession Plan. Most small business owners, as well as their attorneys and accountants, consider an entity taxed as an S-Corporation to be the simplest entity structure to understand and operate. An entity taxed as an S-Corporation offers these benefits:

- Shareholders can receive treatment as W2 employees of the Business

- A shareholder receives their pro rata share of profits/losses and stock appreciation as a matter of law

- S-Corporations escape the double-taxation of a C-Corporation and, in most states, profits flow through to owners at a lower tax rate than wages (a self-employment tax savings)

- Limited liability in certain respects

- Unlimited life—for an S-Corporation with multiple owners, it will continue to exist after the death, withdrawal or departure of any one of the owners

- A tax-conduit or flow-through structure

In most states, there is only one type of corporation recognized and that is what is known as a C-Corporation. When you file *Articles of Incorporation* with your Secretary of State and meet all the basic requirements, your *Articles* are approved and you own a corporation, and technically, it is a C-Corporation. Under federal tax law, however, you can then file Form 2553 within a limited amount of time and elect S-Corporation status. From that point on, the taxing authorities (city, county, state, and federal) will recognize your S-Corporation tax status as long as you continue to qualify. So, technically, a corporation is an entity structure and an S-Corporation is a tax election.

Only certain entities can elect to become an S-Corporation, and they must maintain that status throughout the entire tax year to qualify for the benefits. The business entity must be either a U.S. formed LLC or corporation, cannot have more than 100 shareholders, must have only one class of stock, must distribute profits and losses pro rata to ownership, and all shareholders must be natural persons or qualified trusts, and U.S. citizens or legal residents of the U.S., residing in the U.S. If, for example, one of four shareholders who is a U.S. citizen becomes a resident of a foreign country, the Subchapter S election could terminate, potentially affecting all the shareholders.

One of the most important benefits of an S-Corporation or an LLC/S-Corporation can be self-employment tax (Social Security and Medicare) savings. It is possible, with guidance from your tax advisor, to reasonably divide the business proceeds after expenses are paid into FICA-taxable wages (subject to the many federal, state and local taxes tied to employment compensation and which may also include assessments for unemployment and workers compensation) and FICA-exempt profit distributions. In sum, an S-Corporation only pays wage-based taxes on compensation to its owners, and not on the remaining profits paid out to equity owners as distributions. An S-Corporation must pay a reasonable salary to a shareholder who may also be a W-2 employee. The profits that remain after deducting reasonable compensation and operating expenses is not subject to federal self-employment tax.

Quick aside: Note that city, county, and state taxes can significantly affect the use of an S-Corporation and erode any tax savings. Guidance on this front should come from your local tax advisor before setting up or making an S-Corporation election.

Reasonable compensation is the wage or salary that you pay yourself as a business owner to perform services for your Business before you receive a profit distribution in an S-Corporation or an LLC/S-Corporation. In the simplest of terms, to be considered "reasonable" by the IRS (in hindsight), the amount paid must be equivalent to what a similar business would pay someone else with equivalent qualifications and experience to perform the same or similar services. The IRS looks at many factors to determine if you were paid reasonable compensation if you're audited on this issue, including the nature of the employee's duties, the employee's background and experience, the employee's knowledge of the business, and the size of the business, among other things. By the way, if it isn't clear, the employees in the preceding list are also the owners.

The best way to address this concern is to collaborate with an experienced accountant or attorney and rely on their advice. Another way is to use that Three-Basket Cash Flow System and balance the allocations to each Basket, such as 40/30/30, 35/35/30, or a 35/30/35 cash flow approach (if that doesn't make sense or you're reading these Lessons non-sequentially, please see Lesson Nos. 7 through 9). If profits are divided between two or three owners, you can probably be more aggressive in terms of the amount allocated to profits (e.g., 40/20/40) but, when in doubt, talk to your local tax advisor.

One of the seminal tax cases I remember reading in law school involved an attorney who set up his own S-Corporation and proceeded to pay himself an annual salary of $1.00; everything else, after operating expenses were paid, was taken as profit distribution at the lower tax rate. That approach is a good way to have an IRS case with your name on it forever. Don't do that.

In sum, there are good reasons to set up your business as an LLC or a corporation taxed as an S-Corporation. Younger owners of a minority interest often appreciate the pro rata requirements on their share of the profits and appreciating stock value. There are a couple of draw-backs to be aware of, other than the reasonable compensation issue. First, once you set up an entity and elect S-Corporation taxation, and contribute your Capital Assets into the entity, it will have an ascer-tainable and, perhaps, significant value; if not now, then in the future. Changing from an S-Corporation to an entity taxed as anything else can come with a significant tax bill on what the tax authorities often consider a liquidation event. Second, as we'll explore in depth in the next Lesson, S-Corporations cannot easily onboard next generation talent, which is the ability to trade a Book owner's clients, cash flow, and goodwill for stock via a tax-neutral exchange.

LESSON NO. 14:
ENTITY STRUCTURING CHOICES
(THE HYBRID MODEL)

In the previous two Lessons, we explored and examined the benefits offered through an LLC/Partnership and, separately, the benefits offered through use of an S-Corporation or an LLC/S-Corporation. This Lesson focuses on the unique strategy of using an LLC/Partnership entity structure in conjunction with a series of satellite Member S-Corporations, or LLC/S-Corporations, to provide the combined benefits of both entities to the owners of a single Business (see *Figure 10*). Professional Service Businesses benefit from the tax efficiencies offered by an S-Corporation, but the owners of that same Business may also want to reserve the future ability to onboard Book owners into ownership in a tax-neutral manner. This is the only model that can do both.

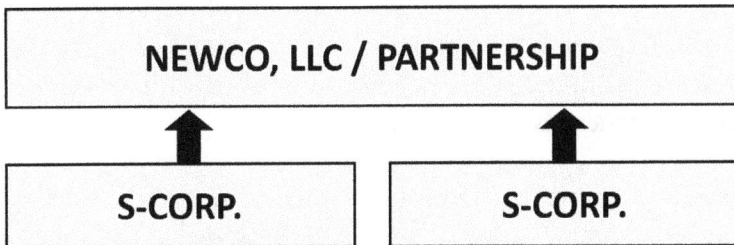

Figure 10

As explained in Lesson No. 2, it is a common truth that many PSPs are Book builders, sole proprietorships, or individuals working alone. By carefully selecting the right entity in advance, this fact can greatly benefit the formation of your Successor Team for your Succession Plan.

The need for qualified, capable, ownership ready, next generation talent (G2s and G3s) to join an existing Practice or Business cannot be overstated. One way to do this, of course, is to recruit, hire, train and promote the talent from within. The problem is that this process takes time and may result in frequent misfires, which can be expensive and time consuming. Another way, and the subject of this Lesson, is to merge in talent who know what it is like to be an owner and have demonstrated that they are willing to take the risk of ownership.

The mechanics at this point may start to sound familiar. Once a good fit is established and due diligence is complete, a Book owner who wants to join an existing Business and its Successor Team signs a *Contribution Agreement*, an *Assignment & Assumption Agreement*, and a *Bill of Sale*, (among other necessary documents) and contributes all rights, title and interest in their clients, related cash flow, and goodwill to Newco, LLC/Partnership. Newco then reciprocates and issues a certain amount of stock (from authorized but unissued shares) to the incoming contributor of roughly equal value to the assets (valuations are commonly performed on both parties or both sides of the transaction immediately before such an event). This is the process that we call onboarding.

One of the unique traits of Partnership tax law is that this onboarding maneuver can be done privately without having to file formal statutory merger documentation. LLC/Partnerships are uniquely well situated to do this, and it can be accomplished with multiple Book builders or owners over the years.

In contrast, statutory mergers are conducted under the rules of the Internal Revenue Code (IRC) Section 368, as well as applicable state statutes. The statutory merger process, is often complicated, time-consuming, and expensive. It generally requires that the sole proprietor Book owner first organize as an entity similar to the Business they want to merge into and then, after a waiting period, file Articles of Merger and/or a Plan of Merger that must be approved by the state in which each entity is organized or incorporated. If you go down this path, in order to avoid a step transaction, be sure to memorialize the independent business purpose that underlies the Book owner's decision to form a new company.

The most common type of "merger" between PSPs is the Tax-Neutral Exchange ("TNE") process. If you are currently organized (or could reorganize) as an LLC taxed as a Partnership, IRC §721 allows for a TNE of assets (from the Book owner) for equity (from the acquiring Business) rather than a formal, statutory merger. A Business in this setting is essentially acquiring a Book of clients and cash flow in exchange for newly issued equity and no cash. In effect, an informal merger of interests. A detailed example of this Tax-Neutral Exchange process is provided in the next Lesson, *How Stock is Bought, Sold, or Exchanged.*

The onboarding of a smaller Book or Practice owner into a larger Business with a strong, sustainable rate of growth and consistent profit distributions paid to the equity partners is an enticing proposition. It is the perfect set of answers as to why an individual Book builder might give up *the going it alone route* and being in near total control of their own Book to become a smaller part of a larger team, and even to take on debt to buy additional Equity as part of a Succession Plan. If the Book owner is in their late twenties to late thirties, for example, and the geography works, you can onboard talent directly into a G2 or G3 slot on your Successor Team using nothing but Equity.

Building on this unique application of an LLC/Partnership, which can accommodate a variety of owners (i.e., individuals, corporations, etc.) this final entity consideration is a hybrid model that blends the best of both worlds. This Hybrid Entity Structure is the most powerful and adaptive vehicle available to a Professional Services owner/ownership group, but it requires multiple entities to achieve these cumulative benefits, making this simultaneously the most complicated and sophisticated of the entity structuring options.

Essentially, the operating entity or the "mothership" is an LLC/Partnership and each owner or partner holds their shares of the LLC/Partnership through their own, privately held S-Corporation, or LLC/S-Corporation, usually domiciled at their respective home offices/addresses. This "satellite" member S-Corporation or LLC/S-Corporation may also include a spouse, child, or others as owners, as well as other business activities, subject to any licensing or regulatory board requirements—possibilities that don't exist at the mothership level. This Hybrid Model requires support from an experienced tax advisor and possibly a tax attorney to organize it all, but once in place it offers the flexibility and onboarding abilities of an LLC/Partnership with the W2 compensation and potential tax efficiencies of an S-Corporation. There is simply no other way to have all these benefits in one business structure.

The take-away of these entity structuring Lessons is that you need to make a determination and set up an entity for where your business is going and what you expect or need it to do for you and your future partners, not where you're at now or even next year. This is ten to twenty-year planning and thinking. Supporting a Succession Plan with next generation owners investing their Books and/or their future profit dollars in a tax efficient manner is challenging, to say the least. But it is also very doable. Think about it carefully, ask lots of questions, and then make your own decision. If your tax and/or legal counsel have little to no experience in documenting and cash flowing a Succession Plan, and/or utilizing such a sophisticated entity structure, then you have to be your own expert. Keep reading, please. Your toolbox should be getting heavier.

LESSON NO. 15:
HOW STOCK IS BOUGHT, SOLD, OR EXCHANGED

In an Equity transaction between a G1 founder and a G2 prospective owner, there are actually three participants involved when viewed through the lens of a Business—the individual seller, the individual buyer, and the entity. Newco, the entity participant, presents numerous intriguing options and alternatives that every business owner should be familiar with. These are useful *tools in the toolbox*; you just need to know how and when to use them.

In the Succession Plans that we are considering throughout the Lessons in this book, the basic rule is that individuals buy Equity and individuals sell Equity. In fact, this is how most Equity transactions work. To be clear, Equity in this context refers to shares of stock that one owns in a Business, or Newco, in this case.

But it is also possible to have a new owner (G2) buy stock directly from Newco, though this functionality usually does not make sense for a host of reasons. For starters, the payment for such Equity would flow into Newco's primary checking account where it can be disbursed as wages or profits at ordinary income tax rates rather than at long-term capital gains rates, offset by any basis, as in the case of an individual seller. Newco may have a need for such funds, for instance, to finance an acquisition, to repay company debt, to pay its bills or to enhance business liquidity. If such is the case, Newco would issue shares to the individual buyer, putting more shares into play and effectively diluting everyone's ownership. If G1 was the 100% owner holding 1,000,000 authorized and issued shares, Newco's issuance of, for example, 100,000 previously authorized but unissued shares to G2 at Fair Market Value means G1 now owns 1,000,000 shares out of 1,100,000 issued shares. G1 has sold no Equity, receives no money from the transaction (at least not directly), and yet is diluted and now a 90% owner, which affects their pro rata profit distributions and stock appreciation rights.

In the right circumstances, such a transaction might increase the value of the Business, but G1 is almost always more inclined to take payment in full as an individual seller at long-term capital gains tax rates. If the Business needs the money, G1 can always lend it and receive interest on the money.

It is also possible for G1 to sell their stock back to Newco over the course of a Succession Plan, provided we're talking about a valuable, profitable, growing Business with more than one owner and, preferably, more than one generation of ownership (that still only takes two people!). Newco can buy, or redeem, a current owner's equity, subject to statutory guardrails usually concerning solvency and liquidity issues. The legal term of art is "a stock redemption." Newco then pays for the equity out of its retained earnings, cash flow or with a bank loan (likely to be guaranteed by G1 in our working fact pattern in this Lesson). The Equity in such a transaction is effectively taken out of circulation and is now authorized but unissued stock. One way to think of this is anti-dilution. To better explain the mechanics of these stock transactions, let's reset the table.

At the time Newco, LLC, is filed and initially set up, the supporting documentation should include some specific adjustments, or additions, to the typical LLC to accommodate the strategies involved in a Succession Plan and this exploration:

1.   Authorize 2,000,000 shares of voting stock

2. Issue 1,000,000 shares of that voting stock to the founders and any other immediate owners

3. Install a Board of Directors (called a Manager-managed LLC in most states and covered in Lesson No. 24)

4. Elect tax treatment as an LLC/Partnership

Quick (detailed) aside: To clarify a couple of key points before proceeding, 2,000,000 shares are authorized and half of that, 1,000,000 shares, are issued, leaving 1,000,000 shares authorized but unissued—these terms (issued and unissued) really matter as we work through the concepts and the mechanics of the process. The reason for authorizing and issuing 1,000,000 shares of stock upon setup (as opposed to 100 shares or 1,000 shares) is to reduce the price per share to single or double digits, so that in the first Tranche or two, at least, shares can be bought, sold or exchanged with greater precision (i.e., no fractional interests). Technically, an LLC/Partnership can create additional shares easily at any time but from a learning perspective, we will keep applying those corporate attributes and master the concepts first.

Now that the table has been set, let us get back to the stock redemption process so you can determine if this tool makes sense for you and your Business. When G1 begins the first Tranche of the Succession Plan and they sell 100,000 shares of their Equity Interest to G2, G1's Equity Interest decreases to 900,000 shares and G2's Equity Interest increases to 100,000 shares. G2 obtains a conventional bank loan to pay for the stock. We still have the same 1,000,000 shares authorized and issued, or outstanding, in a single-class structure. And we still have the original 1,000,000 shares of authorized but unissued stock for potential future transactions or exchanges. This is a common first step, or Tranche, in a Succession Plan.

Now let us add a stock redemption event to the fact pattern. Newco, LLC, is our buyer. Let us make this transaction subsequent to G1's sale of stock to G2 by ten years and assume that two more next generation owners have also acquired Equity in the meantime. The current ownership structure, ten years down the road, is

60%/20%/10%/10%, G1/G2(A)/G2(B)/G2(C) respectively, with 1,000,000 shares authorized and issued to the four owners (see *Figure 11*). For whatever reason, G1 suddenly wants to fully retire and cash out their remaining Equity. To do this via stock redemption, Newco acquires all of G1's 600,000 shares and returns it to the category of "authorized but unissued". Newco now has 400,000 shares issued, all held by the G2s, with Newco holding 1,600,000 shares of unissued stock (unissued shares have no impact on share value). The new ownership structure is now 0%/50%/25%/25%, G1/G2(A)/G2(B)/G2(C) respectively. (G2(A) now owns 200,000 shares out of 400,000 shares authorized and issued, G2(B) owns 100,000 shares out of 400,000, and so on. Each of the G2 owners are anti-diluted proportionally.

The foregoing example is offered to help you understand the basic mechanics, and to highlight some of the less obvious ramifications. G1's sudden desire to cash out and retire will probably trigger the terms of a Buy-Sell Agreement and that may result in a discount to G1's sale price. The sudden nature of the event may also mean that Newco is the financially strongest and

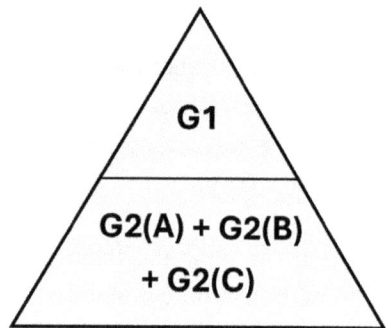

Figure 11

most capable buyer, especially if any of the G2s recently bought their Equity. In addition and in contrast to all three of the G2s buying Equity from G1 upon their retirement, it takes only one transaction via stock redemption to change the ownership positions of four individuals. Of course, the G2s will receive a substantial increase in their share of any profit distributions and place the entirety of the debt obligation on Newco's Balance Sheet, all good reasons to consider this maneuver. To be clear, the use of stock redemption can be the right tool to do the job; it is by no means an anomaly in the world of succession planning.

There are downsides to be aware of. For one, Newco's payment of FMV (perhaps with a discount) to G1 for the redemption and purchase of their 600,000 shares is not tax deductible to the Buyer; there is no Cost Basis accrued. This creates Phantom Income to the remaining owners pro rata who will pay taxes on money they don't receive (i.e., the money used to retire the debt and/or pay off G1). The Successor Team members all become larger owners of Newco, without writing any individual checks, but there is still a cost. If Newco was required to obtain bank financing, each of the G2s will probably be required to personally guarantee Newco's Promissory Note. Finally, the Successor Team members acquire no individual Basis even though they are responsible for servicing the bank loan or seller financed note.

On a different tack and building on the previous Lesson where the Hybrid Entity Structure was introduced, another exception to the individual seller to individual buyer rule is when a younger Book owner decides they want to join a larger Business and be part of its Succession Plan. Book Owner agrees to sign a Contribution Agreement, among other documents, in favor of Newco, LLC, taxed as a Partnership, executing a Tax-Neutral Exchange. The basics of this procedure, called an onboarding process, were covered in the previous Lesson.

Let's reset the table one more time and get into the details of the onboarding process. G1 owns 900,000 shares and G2 owns 100,000 shares, and we have another 1,000,000 shares of authorized but unissued stock in reserve. G1 and G2 talk to the younger Book Owner and, after sufficient due diligence, the decision is made to proceed. A qualified appraiser values Newco, and separately, the Book to be contributed. Simple division provides one answer, price vs. value another answer, and negotiations determine how much Equity the new Book owner will receive for their contribution. Let's say it is 5%, or 50,000 shares (not accounting for any dilution to keep it simple).

The Book Owner contributes their Capital Assets as an individual to Newco. Newco, in effect, trades the Book Owner for their assets, completing the exchange with 50,000 shares of newly issued stock from Newco. This is one example of why we authorize more shares than we initially issue and is the reason we need an LLC taxed as a Partnership (this is much more difficult in an S-Corporation setting). At this time, Newco now has 1,050,000 shares authorized and issued with G1 still owning 900,000 shares, G2 still owning 100,000 shares and the former Book Owner, now a New Owner, holding 50,000 shares.

G1 and G2 have not sold any of their Equity and, accordingly, have no tax liability, but everyone, even New Owner, are diluted pro rata by the issuance of the additional 50,000 shares. While dilution is often frowned upon by owners and thought of as something to be avoided, this story has a positive aspect. The contribution of the Book Owner's Capital Assets to Newco's Balance Sheet should increase the value of the Business immediately, tax free and debt free, and therefore positively affect shareholders' value.

This example also illustrates why a one-class Equity system can be beneficial. Even though New Owner received newly issued shares of stock from Newco, their shares are exactly the same in all respects as G1's and G2's shares. Our new 5% owner will now immediately share in the profits of the Business as well as its stock appreciation, pro rata (more likely than not). And our New Owner will receive compensation for the work they do (from Basket No. 2). These cumulative benefits are what prompt next generation Book owners to enter into an onboarding maneuver.

A common and usually simultaneous event when New Owner completes their Tax-Neutral Exchange is that the 5% owner will seek to acquire more stock to solidify their place as a member of the Successor Team and to acquire stock at the lowest possible price available, which is "Now!" in a fast-growing Business. That stock will come from G1 in an individual to individual transaction, with our New Owner likely obtaining a conventional bank loan to pay for the Equity Interest at FMV. Note that if the New Owner buys another 50,000 shares, they will receive 10% of the profit distributions from Basket No. 3 to pay for an acquisition of half that amount. Even on an after-tax basis, that math generally works out quite well provided that the Business continues to grow. With a third motivated owner helping, that should be everyone's expectation.

This Lesson illustrates the interplay between the Business and its underlying entity structure, and the individual shareholders of that Business. Some of this might seem complicated and *a bridge too far*, but in my world, the steps explored in this Lesson happen every single day. This is succession planning at its finest!

LESSON NO. 16: GRANTING AND GIFTING STOCK

I believe that stock, or any form of Equity, in a valuable Professional Services Business should never be treated like a birthday present. Do not give it away. Closely held, restricted and regulated stock has as many continuing obligations as it does opportunities. Owners of Equity in the context of a Succession Plan should be actively involved in the success and growth of the Business; that requires an investment mindset. That said, I'll explain the mechanics of the process and you, having earned the right to make your own business decisions, can decide what to do with this information.

First of all, granting and gifting are not the same things. A grant of stock is synonymous with the granting of a cash bonus at year end for a job well done. A cash bonus, basically a "grant of cash", takes the form of a check or ACH payroll transfer and, of course, comes from Newco's checking account. As the money leaves Newco's checking account, it is deducted as an ordinary business expense. As it arrives in the hands or the bank account of the happy employee, it is usually on a W2 basis and taxed accordingly. A grant of stock, or a stock bonus, works the same way except that it has many additional qualifications and complications built in.

A grant of stock, just like granting a cash bonus, is an action taken by the business, by Newco, LLC in our example. It is not an individual to individual transaction. Newco takes authorized but unissued stock (as we worked with in the previous Lesson) and bestows it on a worthy recipient, usually a key employee, perhaps a son or daughter. As the previously unissued stock is issued, it's value (best determined by an appraiser) is generally deductible by Newco as an ordinary business expense. As that stock, or Equity, is received by a key employee, a myriad of things could happen and this is where stock grants become complex.

Technically, the value of a grant is taxed to the recipient on an ordinary income basis but, as I like to say, "It depends." In the case of a stock grant, it depends on the issues of vesting, valuation, discounting, tax deferral, tax acceleration, the terms of the Buy-Sell Agreement (i.e., can the recipient cash in the grant a month later?), voting rights, continuing employment, and governance, and that's the short list. Working with closely held, restricted stock means all the details have to be considered and memorialized. Stock can certainly be granted, but it has to be done properly and usually with professional guidance.

Gifting is quite different. Under the IRC, the IRS defines a gift as "proceeds from 'detached and disinterested generosity,' ... 'out of affection, respect, admiration, charity or like impulses." Established law states that this test or threshold cannot be met when an employer gifts stock to an employee. A gift, if it meets the IRC criteria to be a gift, is not taxable to the recipient. Stock gifted to an employee, or a son or daughter who is an employee of the business is a taxable event, effectively a grant with all the attendant rules.

Estate plans that involve family members is yet a different situation and goes well beyond the focus of this book. Gifting in the context of a family estate plan is possible with the help and guidance of professionals, but having participated in a handful of transactions, I can tell you that it is not easy or inexpensive. If interested, start by talking to your estate planning legal counsel and your tax counsel. You'll also need a formal appraisal to establish the value of the stock as of the date of the gift, for starters. It might make sense given your circumstances, but it is always on a case-by-case basis.

For the past 30 years (including my time as a securities attorney), I have been assisting Professional Services owners with their Succession Plans, each involving multiple Tranches and more than a thousand individual transactions. We used stock grants maybe half a dozen times in 30 years. In each instance, however, the grants occurred before the founding owner asked for direction or permission—they just did it and ignored the tax consequences. I remember one of their local CPA's saying on a conference call after he found out, several years later, "OK, but don't ever do that again!" Three of the succession plans involved formal estate planning coordinated gifts to family members or charities, complete with IRS-specific appraisals, and tax attorneys to guide the process from start to finish. Again, it is certainly doable if you are determined and it makes financial sense; just plan ahead as it takes some time.

I would like to conclude by telling you that grants and gifts typically aren't necessary to complete a Succession Plan, but that's not really fair to the handful of successful, more valuable Businesses, family or otherwise, where it might be helpful and financially advantageous. I'll concede on that point and try to offer some practical solutions with the remainder of this Lesson. Small business owners can always find a way!

When considering granting or gifting strategies, there is often a common, simpler, safer approach that Professional Service owners can use and it falls under the heading of "timing is everything." Once Newco, LLC, is filed and set up, with assets contributed into it, a bank account opened, a TIN/EIN obtained, the rules change tax-wise. At this point going forward, Newco has an ascertainable value and share price. When Newco grants or gifts shares to a key employee or other individual, the general rule, as you have learned, is that the recipient is taxed as ordinary income on the valued shares, treating it as a form of compensation unless there is an exception or exclusion in the IRC.

The point is this—before Newco is filed and fully set up, the rules are different. When setting up Newco, before any valued or valuable assets are contributed into the new entity, one can justifiably argue that the shares of stock in Newco are worthless as the business does not own any assets and has no operations. At this juncture, other prospective owners such as key employees, an associated Book builder, a son, a daughter, etc., with something to contribute (i.e., goodwill, a client list, a desk and a chair) can do so for a small but reasonable amount of Equity in Newco received in exchange and likely avoid any compensation/tax issues.

I often teach this concept with a bit more color. Once a circus tent is set up and all the edges are staked down tight, the only way in is through the ticket line. There is a cost to enter. But if one is helping to set the circus tent up and is inside when the edges are secured, well, there is no need to buy a ticket and pay the entrance fee. You are already inside! I am quite sure an IRS Agent would find a different way to describe the process, as would your CPA, but this is my experience under the watchful eyes of accountants across the country. It works.

If you are intent on "granting" stock, this is the time, place, and method to do it—after obtaining the approval of your CPA to be sure. Tax avoidance can never be the sole reason. If there is a legitimate business reason and a logical, defendable purpose, this is a way to get the job done safely in most cases. It is common that some Professional Service venues have regulatory constraints on who can own Equity as well, so always be sure to know your rules.

And with that, if you are still adamant about including formal grants and/or gifts as part of your Succession Plan, you will probably need to read someone else's book for more of the how-to details.

LESSON NO. 17:
USING VOTING AND
NON-VOTING STOCK

Many of the local business attorneys that I work with, or who enter into the succession planning process invited in by their G1 client, recommend that their client (G1(s)) only sell non-voting stock to the Successor Team (G2s and G3s). Even in the strict confines of S-Corporation rules, the use of non-voting stock does not create a second class of Equity as long as that is the *only* difference. Specifically, G1 might own 800,000 shares of voting stock in Tranche One and G2(A) and G2(B) each own 100,000 shares of non-voting stock in a single class equity system. For this strategy to make sense, however, think about ten to fifteen years later when G1, in their sixties, backed up by a complete Successor Team, now owns just 40% of the Equity Interests, but all the voting stock.

The local attorneys are not wrong but, in my experience, their advice is impractical and a bit too simplistic in most cases. In fairness, and as a past practicing attorney myself, your legal counsel has one job, and that is to zealously advocate for your interests; to protect you. To keep you safe and in full control, it is standard practice to recommend limiting voting stock to just the founder(s). The other owners certainly receive all the financial and tax benefits of being an owner, as the argument goes, but they do not get to vote or a voice as a shareholder unless and until G1 chooses otherwise. This is good advice by good attorneys doing their job, at least at first glance.

Here is the problem that arises in the field. Even though the IRS says that non-voting stock is not, for that reason alone, a second class of stock, next generation investors, along with their own legal and tax counsel, and often their lenders, feel like it is and argue accordingly. Giving you a preview of the next Lesson, this is one of those places where price lags value. In other words, the two dozen times I've worked with succession planning clients and the non-voting stock path was followed, or attempted, the G2 prospective owners argued for a very large discount on the per-share price of the Equity they were considering buying—enough that each deal either failed or G1 realized that there were other and better ways to retain control *and* obtain full value.

In our example above, if G1 owns 800,000 shares of voting stock in a single-class entity structure, and G2(A) owns 100,000 voting shares, and G2(B) owns 100,000 voting shares, G1 will win every single shareholder vote for which the voting threshold is 80% or less (and very few, if any, decisions are set at more than 80%). Practically, small businesses with less than five or six owners and one dominant (51%+) owner rarely, if ever, vote their shares of stock or Equity. There would be no point. Add in G1's role as CEO and as a Board member and there is little chance that the founder's ability to exert near total control is in jeopardy.

As mentioned above, where it gets more interesting is when, in later Tranches, G1 owns less than 51% of the authorized and issued shares of stock but is still the single, largest shareholder. An ownership structure of 40%/30%/30%, G1/G2(A)/G2(B) respectively, demonstrates this numerically. Acting in unison, the Successor Team could outvote the founder. Some G1s choose to retain a 51% interest until they formally retire, selling the rest or most of their remaining shares to the Successor Team members at that time. Other G1s choose to retain their position as CEO and as Chairperson of the Board with final say memorialized on a list of key business decisions and maintain control in this manner.

Control of a business matters a lot to almost every G1 I've ever worked with. G2's will care at some point, but I often counsel them that, at least in the early Tranches, *the ability to influence can be as important as the ability to control.* It's nice to have the ear of the boss/founder, but not to have their burdens of ownership and leadership.

> **Quick aside:** A number of the strategic Succession Planning steps that we cover in this book rely on the use of an LLC that elects to be taxed as a Partnership. In this particular tax structure, an LLC can have as many classes of Equity as the G1 owner(s) want. It is a benefit that may not be needed in the near term, but in a Business that doubles in size a couple of times and has ten or more owners in the coming years, the time may well come when a second class solves more problems than it creates.

My advice is to only issue voting stock and read Lesson Nos. 24 and 25 if control or a voice in governance is an issue that you have serious concerns about now, or later when you are closer to retirement.

LESSON NO. 18:
UNDERSTANDING BUSINESS
VALUE AND VALUATION

Respectfully, for all you may know about business value and valuation approaches, the value of your business is not what you think. That is a universal truth I've observed first-hand over the past 30-plus years in the M&A space (unless your profession involves valuing businesses!). I like to say that half of the owners I've dealt with underestimate the value of what they've built, half overestimate their value, and each half thinks that the other half is applying the wrong rules and logic to the process. Let's explore some important basics and learn something more together.

Most small business owners have some idea of what their Business or Practice is worth, though most estimates are based on rules of thumb which look at just one of perhaps a hundred variables and try to draw a useful conclusion. Frankly, I did that all the time in my own Business just to keep a sense of perspective. At the same time, I'd never be able to sell stock or obtain a bank loan without a formal business appraisal. I get it, sometimes when you're out hiking, it pays to get out your GPS and let the satellites tell you exactly where you are; other times it is enough to look around and get your bearings in a simpler way. It depends on how mission critical it is that you know exactly where you're at—or to put it more bluntly, where someone else thinks you're at.

I'm going to say this a couple of times because owners need to hear it: the only way to know what your business is worth for the specific purpose you have in mind is to have it valued by a professionally qualified and objective Appraiser. Everything else is just a guess. There will be a difference in opinion between owner and Appraiser—count on it. Sometimes that difference is many times the cost of the valuation you might be avoiding and is in your favor (i.e., your rule of thumb came in way too low). Sometimes reading an appraisal report feels like your ship just ran aground on a rocky shoal. Like it or not, you need to know the facts and the valuation logic at some point as they apply to what you are building.

The first thing to know is that Professional Service businesses don't have just one value, and there is no single valuation approach or method that can be applied to every situation or Business. Just like with your car, value depends on the purpose of the valuation. Are you valuing your car to sell it to a third-party? To trade it in? Are you donating it to charity? Are you liquidating the asset at the end of its useful life? Depending on the purpose, your car can have many different values across a wide range, and the values can all be correct. Business valuations work the same way, especially when considering the difference between selling assets to an outside buyer (i.e., an Exit Plan) or when selling a non-controlling equity interest to a next generation owner/investor (i.e., as part of a Succession Plan).

Traditionally, there are three valuation approaches, and several predominant methods under each approach that are used to determine value depending on your specific purpose:

- **Income Approach**
  - Capitalization of Cash Flows
  - Discounted Cash Flow Method

- **Market Approach**
  - Guideline Transaction Method
  - Direct Market Data Method

- **Asset Approach**
  - Book Value
  - Adjusted Net Asset Value Method

In addition to these professional approaches and methods, on the practical side of things, Books and even one-owner Practices are often valued using a multiple of gross revenue or a GRM, which is a rule of thumb. One example of a GRM is valuing a Professional Services Book or Practice at 1.0 x T12 (trailing twelve months) gross revenue. The gross revenue multiple in this example is 1.0, and depending on your profession and cash flow, GRM's often range from 0.80 up to 3.00. Back in my day as an attorney with a small Book, for instance, I sold for a GRM of 1.0 x T12 using an earn-out arrangement.

A GRM is often used on smaller cash flow streams, think $250,000/ year or less, where the logic in avoiding a formal appraisal lies somewhere between, "How wrong can I be?!", and "I'm not paying someone $8,000 to tell me what I already know!" Books and Practices don't sell their expenses and potential liabilities to an outside or third-party buyer; that and the lower revenue sometimes negates the need for an appraisal. And even if you own a larger and more sophisticated Business and you just want to satisfy your curiosity, a GRM appropriate for your line of work may be good enough (though an earnings-based multiple is still more appropriate). If you want to sell your entire Practice or Book and gross more than about $250,000/ year, and especially if the buyer wants to obtain a bank loan to cash you out, a simple rule of thumb usually needs to yield to a formal valuation performed by a licensed, qualified Appraiser. The lender will decide the issue for everyone involved. And if you're selling restricted stock in your regulated Professional Services Business to a younger investor, you need an objective, professional opinion of value, every time.

One of the common ways to value a Business is to calculate its Fair Market Value (FMV)—a term you will read throughout this book. FMV is defined by the American Society of Appraisers as *"The amount at which a property would change hands between a willing buyer and a willing seller, neither being under any compulsion to buy or to sell, and both having reasonable knowledge of relevant facts."* FMV is a standard of value, or the definition of value that is being measured by an Appraiser.

In the simplest of terms, Synergistic Value refers to the extra value created when two businesses merge or collaborate, surpassing the sum of their combined, individual values. Intrinsic Value refers to the actual value of a business's assets, calculated based on its underlying business fundamentals, independent of its market value. In essence, it is a long-term perspective on a company's value, focusing on its ability to generate cash flow over time. Investment Value reflects the value that an investor is willing to pay to obtain an asset or investment based on that buyer's subjective goals, beliefs, and criteria. It can be higher or lower than market value depending on the investor's unique circumstances and perspective. I've reduced tomes to a couple of short phrases here, but the take away is that FMV, the most commonly applied standard, may place a lower value on a business than when using one of these other standards. When an Appraiser is hired, you need to talk about the standard of value to be used.

With all this on the table, let's put things back into perspective. Think back to Lesson No. 7, the Three-Basket Cash Flow System, where we examined how a strong Business can bring as much as 25% (or more) of annual gross revenue to the bottom line after all expenses and owners' compensation has been paid. Using $1,000,000 in gross revenue, this leaves $250,000 in actual profits (Basket No. 3). Starting here, let's talk about the valuation differences between a Succession Plan and an Exit Plan, because they are significant.

> **Quick aside:** As I mentioned earlier, and in case you're not reading these Lessons sequentially, if you are an owner of a Professional Services model that has much higher overhead and, as a result, profits in the 8% to 15% range, please understand that the Lessons and logic still apply, just to a smaller bottom line. It isn't about how one Professional Services venue compares to another; it is about how different Businesses in the same profession

or field of work compare. Professional Service Businesses with 10% profitability as an industry norm, who manage their cash flows well and are more profitable than average, will probably be more valuable than average.

A Succession Plan usually requires next generation owners to acquire a non-controlling Equity Interest, buying in with after-tax dollars, and buying in to the existing Profit & Loss Statement and the existing Balance Sheet. New owners, G2s in our parlance, buy expenses and liabilities. For these reasons, among others, the profits of $250,000 earned from $1,000,000 in gross revenue, in this continuing example, are often valued in the range of 4 to 6 times EBITDA, using a simple, rule-of-thumb multiple of earnings. That's a rough valuation range of $1,000,000 to $1,500,000 for many, but not all, Professional Service Businesses. Of course, your specific profession, location, competition, niche, and growth rates also matter—a lot. Note that a formal valuation properly looks at dozens of factors rather than just one thing like your earnings.

Let's compare and contrast the Succession Plan route to that of an Exit Plan. An Exit Plan allows, in most cases, a stronger, larger buyer to avoid acquiring the seller's expenses and liabilities and, when structured correctly, to write off or depreciate the entire purchase price over time. These are some significant advantages over the younger G2 buyer/investor with little personal capital to invest. The result is that buyers or acquirers often pay a multiple of earnings in an Exit Plan format of 7 to 9 times EBITDA, sometimes even higher in an organized market (but often closer to the 7x number than the 10x number, not to get your hopes up).

You knew it was coming, but here is the caveat. These valuation ranges and rules of thumb are simply not reliable across the vast spectrum of Professional Service Business models and venues and locations. This is a learning experience and the concepts are sound; but real numbers depend on specific facts and details. The need to shift to a bottom-line mentality for value and valuation purposes, as a Business owner or builder, is the other takeaway.

So, why would G1 want to sell their Equity Interest for a 4x or 5x EBITDA multiple through a Succession Plan when they could sell at a 7x or 8x multiple through an Exit Plan? The simple answer starts with this formula, with results derived over at least ten years as G1 gradually turns over the workload to their Successor Team:

WAGES + PROFIT DISTRIBUTIONS + EQUITY INCOME + STOCK APPRECIATION

A G1 owner who starts the Succession Planning process early enough can enjoy the cumulative benefits of wages, profits, equity income and stock appreciation, the accompanying tax efficiencies, all while reducing time in the office from Tranche-to-Tranche. Most founders find this approach, along with the control factor, to be more lucrative than selling for a lump sum to an outside buyer. (Read Lesson No. 32 and you'll see this Shareholder Value equation get even better!)

Last thoughts:

1. The level of profitability dictates Business value; those same profits are used to service the debt when G2 buys in and that is not a coincidence.

2. This would be a suitable time to review Lesson No. 9 on the concept of Shareholder Value

3. Have your business valued once "for practice" before you do it (for the first time) for a really important purpose. Appraisals and the valuation process are not intuitive, they're not enjoyable, but are very necessary.

And one more time: The only way to know what your Business is worth for the purpose you have in mind is to have it valued by a professionally qualified and objective Appraiser.

A lot to think about here and this was the simple version. Thanks for reading. Take a break—you'll need it for the next Lesson!

LESSON NO. 19:
SYNTHETIC EQUITY

Synthetic Equity is a way to provide your key employees with some of the economic benefits of ownership without actual stock, or Equity, changing hands. Most business owners have at least a passing familiarity with the basic concept already. Common approaches include phantom stock, stock appreciation rights, a long-term incentive plan, a profits interest, and a significant bonus that pays out only at the end of an employee's career based on the company's value or success, to name just a few. Note that these terms of art have specific meanings and each must be used correctly under the law and the IRC.

Briefly, here is how Synthetic Equity works. Think of this horizontal line as the complete spectrum from compensation at one end, to equity at the other end (see *Figure 12*).

As for the far left of this spectrum, think of a traditional W2 base wage plus a variable or discretionary bonus paid quarterly or annually based on metrics agreed upon by employer and employee—perhaps what you're already doing for your key employees. On the far right,

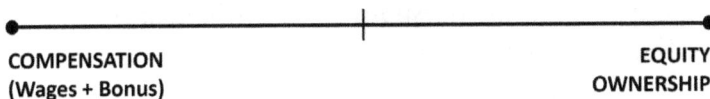

COMPENSATION
(Wages + Bonus)

EQUITY
OWNERSHIP

Figure 12

think generally of shares of stock in Newco, LLC ("Newco"), electing to be taxed as a Partnership or an S-Corporation, and specifically of a G2 owner who buys a 10% Equity Interest in Newco. Effectively, everything in between the left dot and the right dot is where Synthetic Equity exists or can exist if you're so inclined and creative enough. Synthetic Equity is something less than Equity ownership with all its attendant benefits and obligations, and it is something more than a base wage plus a bonus. That's a lot of territory to work with.

Owning stock in a small business provides the owner or investor with a *bundle of rights* that include a voice in the governance and operations, cost basis, a share of profit distributions, stock appreciation benefits, limited liability, the ability to sell the Equity at long-term capital gains tax rates, and more. What many owners don't realize is that this bundle of rights is severable. Synthetic Equity works with one or two of these rights and fashions a tax-compliant, motivational long-term benefit or compensation package for one or more key employees.

A Succession Plan requires next generation owners to make an actual investment in Equity ownership, often a career-length obligation, and there is no substitute for that. G1s and G2s exist to the far right of this spectrum. So, why are we talking about this concept then? Synthetic Equity typically plays no role in obtaining Equity in a Business unless it provides convertible interests earned synthetically—not a common feature in most Succession Plans.

We're introducing this concept to you because there is also no substitute for treating key employees "like owners" and providing needed recognition and monetary rewards to keep the entire team together, in support of a valuable, profitable, and sustainable Business and its ownership team. Synthetic Equity has its place and you need only know enough to ask the questions and start investigating the possibilities. This is another tool in the toolbox.

Start with the basic fact that Equity ownership in a small business just isn't for everyone. Add in the notion of a ten-year amortized, personally guaranteed conventional loan to service the debt for a minority interest, and Equity ownership in a small business is for a relatively small, select group. Synthetic Equity, in all its various forms, tends to offer key employees "ownership like benefits" without the attendant debt obligations. The catch is that key employees are required to contribute their best efforts in helping the Business grow and/or achieve specific objectives; and the key employee needs to be there when the reward payment is made or due, making *tenure* part of the quid pro quo. Meanwhile, actual Equity is reserved for those investors who are willing and able to take the risk of buying into ownership.

A qualified plan designer can tailor Synthetic Equity to match the scope of individual team members and their contributions, making it an effective tool for a variety of roles and responsibilities across a multitude of Professional Service business models. Start by talking to your business attorney and/or CPA and listen to their thinking. Gather all the information you can and then make your own decision.

One last point, regulatory bodies often govern the eligibility of Equity ownership in many Professional Service Businesses. Synthetic Equity is a great alternative for the non-licensed staff members who really make a difference and whose Length of Service (LOS) deserves consideration of something more than the basic wage and bonus reward system. Depending on your choice of entity, Synthetic Equity can offer a vast array of tools to work with. LLC's taxed as Partnerships offer the widest array of options, but even a basic S-Corporation provides good, reliable Synthetic Equity choices.

LESSON NO. 20:
THE CASE FOR MULTIPLE
NEXT GEN OWNERS
(AND OTHER DETAILS)

The basic but important reasons why a Succession Plan includes *multiple* next generation owners on the Successor Team, along with the benefits of the Team members buying in incrementally over several Tranches, are explored in this Lesson which is laid out a little differently in an effort to convey the information. As you'll read, these concepts are actually woven together in the succession planning process. The logic is something like this:

Solving the Continuity Planning Problem. Thinking back to the definition of a Continuity Plan in one of the earlier Lessons, we use a Buy-Sell Agreement to address sudden changes in the ownership team (death, disability, termination of employment status, loss of licensure, etc.). Consider the possibility that, if four or five years into Tranche One (T1), after the Business has grown significantly, G1 has to buy out their only G2 because that G2 owner has a serious health issue, a serious car accident, or just doesn't want to pursue an Equity path any longer, the Succession Plan shifts into reverse. G1 is now buying Equity instead of selling it. The better approach is that each G2 owner needs to participate in a Continuity Plan that relies on *other G2 owners*. Beyond age 50, or so, it usually makes no sense for G1 (or any of the senior owners), to be acquiring Equity from the younger owners, if Succession Planning is the goal. A good rule of thumb is to have two G2s for every G1 owner.

Another option to consider is for G1 to rely on owners outside their Business during the early years of T1, or as long as there is only one G2 owner on the Successor Team. At some point, the sole G2 Successor Team member might prove to be the answer; until then, it is better to be safe on this issue. You can always change your mind and document any obligations accordingly. G2 will likely let you know when they're ready to take on the full obligation and expect that it may not happen until the start of T2—one reason to start the second Tranche before the first one is completed.

Addressing the Issue of Tenure. Many G1s think that the biggest problem to solve for in a Succession Plan is to answer the question, "Where does G2 get the money to buy them out?" But there are good answers for that question (see Lesson Nos. 7, 8 , 21 and 32) and I'd even suggest properly rephrasing the question as "Where does G2 get the money to gradually buy in and service the debt over a long period?" There are even better answers to that question.

Experience dictates that the bigger problem to solve for is actually one of tenure. In other words, how do you get a 30-something-year-old (plus or minus ten years), minority owner of an intangible, Professional Services Business to make the first of a series of career-length investments? And then to do it again, and maybe again?! The fact is not all thirty-something year old G2s or G3s will stick with it. Ownership, and the opportunities and obligations that come with it, is not for everyone. In fairness, we're talking about the single, longest commitment a young, first time owner will make, next to their marriage! Even a thirty-year home mortgage allows for a complete change of residence, or two, or three, along the way.

And sometimes it is the new, younger owner's spouse or significant other that objects to the risk and time horizon of the investment, and they may be right. Having more than one G2 owner not only diversifies the risk that one younger owner might leave, it also serves to create some friendly and good competition and ensures that the best talent is available to serve the clients and to lead the Business in the years to come—not just the oldest member of the Successor Team, or a relative, or the first to purchase Equity.

G2's Perspective. Still on the subjects of multiple next generation owners and their tenure, but looking at it from a different vantage point, let's acknowledge that the process of buying out G1's total Equity Interest over time and paying, in some cases, up to seven figures of total value with after-tax dollars is difficult and expensive. Dividing that task among a group of collaborative younger investors who each buy smaller amounts of Equity over two or three Tranches is smart work and smart investing…and usually very necessary to make the Succession Plan cash flow.

In the end, the second generation of owners may well have an ownership structure (after G1 retires) of 40%/30%/30%, for example. This structure supports three younger owners, all with a minority ownership position, all with seats on the Board of Directors. From this ownership structure, the process of continuity planning and even implementing a third generation of successors becomes much more manageable than buying out a 100%, dominant G1 owner. The journey from the first generation to the second generation is the hardest because, in any given business, it has never been done. The journey from the second generation to the third, and even a fourth generation, has a blueprint to follow, and a culture to guide it.

Also consider that the 40% owner in our example above will probably acquire their total Equity Interest over two or three Tranches. This reduces the total investment per Tranche and gives each member of the Successor Team the opportunity to reassess the opportunity at hand, along with their spouse or significant other. Is there a good reason to buy more Equity? Does the ROI justify the rising Equity price? Looking to the future, is the growth and profitability of the Business sufficient, and sustainable, to support the investment? These are questions to be weighed by increasingly experienced next generation investors as the Succession Plan progresses. They're good questions. The Successor Team isn't obligated to acquire more Equity if they don't think it is wise or is too risky. This isn't one, single, large investment—it is a series of smaller ones with the time to carefully consider each step.

In turn, it takes a strong, well-run Business over many years for the Successor Team members to make it through this gauntlet. At the same time, a G2's Equity Interest very quickly becomes the single, largest, most valuable asset they own, and it is an asset that they are helping to grow—G2s have some control over their own future and wealth.

Pause here, please, and remember that a Succession Plan is designed to build a multi-generational Business by *gradually* transferring ownership and leadership to a team of next generation Equity owners. We defined the term by watching the process unfold in the hands of other Professional Service owners. It is a powerful strategy that takes time to deploy, which is often exactly what G1 wants and the Successor Team needs. If an Exit Plan can be called *fast and complete*, a Succession Plan relies on *slow and steady*. Time is not an adversary; it is an ally.

And under the category of "other details," more of what I've learned over the years…

Non-Revenue Producers and Non-Service Providers. G2 owners, eventually the senior members of your Successor Team, are almost always revenue producers because revenue growth is largely where the money comes from to fuel the debt service on the Equity purchases. Non-revenue producers who play a key role in the Business can certainly be owners as well but tend to be smaller owners (think 3% to 5% of the total ownership picture) and often opt instead for a Synthetic Equity solution (addressed in the preceding Lesson) that provides a wealth building opportunity with no debt service obligation.

But don't assume anything. If you have a loyal, hardworking key employee who really makes a difference, it might just make sense to have a conversation and talk about the opportunity (not an offer) and see what they think. Would they like to be an owner? Are they willing to sign a promissory note, perhaps using friendly, seller financing, to get it done? Would they rather not? I've had some terrific, non-equity "partners" and I think it is important to honor those who helped us get where we are, even if they didn't *put their house on the line* in the early years. That's just not for everyone.

A New HR Team. As the Succession Plan successfully unfolds, and certainly by the time G2(s) buy in again in T2, the responsibility for hiring, training and promoting next generation talent should begin to shift to the senior Successor Team members, with guidance from G1(s) of course. The G3 level of ownership is the future. These are the Business and continuity partners for G2, so it is important to let the G2 owners make some of these decisions, right or wrong. They'll learn, just like you and I did.

Finally, be sure to tell your current hiring prospects during their interviews about your Succession Plan thinking as well. Let them know that this is or will be a part of your Business's culture. This can be an important hiring advantage over one-generational Professional Service Practice models. In this Lesson, we're sharpening the tools already in the toolbox.

LESSON NO. 21:
THE MATH OF A
SUCCESSION PLAN

Good intentions and hard work aside, there is a lot about the succession planning process that comes down to plain and simple math. Nothing is more compelling or convincing to a G2/G3 investor than a ten-year, forward looking, conservative spreadsheet model that clearly paints the picture with no words spoken. Here is what you need to know.

G1's options in their Succession Plan depend on the start date of the Plan and their anticipated retirement date, which may or may not involve completely walking away from the business. It is wise to assume that G1's minimum time commitment in a formal Succession Plan is about ten years. A ten-year commitment by G1 often results in a 15 to 20 year commitment by the G2 buyers of G1's Equity as we will explain. This is step one to understanding the math process.

Let's get specific. Tranche One (T1) may result in a sale of 200,000 shares of G1's

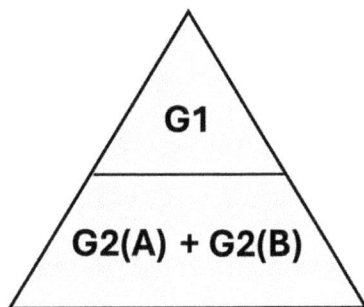

Figure 13

1,000,000 shares of stock to two G2s whom we'll call G2(A) and G2(B), each buying 100,000 shares from G1 on the same date and at the same price per share (see *Figure 13*). This moves ownership from 100% G1 to an 80%/10%/10% ownership structure, G1/G2(A)/G2(B) respectively. G1 collects two checks, based on the Business's FMV at that moment in time, presumably at long-term capital gains tax rates and G2(A) and G2(B) each sign ten-year term notes with a local bank for conventional bank loans at the then applicable interest rates.

Four or five years later, if all is going well, Tranche Two, or T2 is executed. The Business is reappraised at current Fair Market Value (FMV) and G1 sells another 200,000 shares cumulatively to G2(A), G2(B), and a new owner, G2(C), moving ownership from 80%/10%/10%, to 60%/20%/15%/5%, G1/G2(A)/G2(B)/G2(C) respectively (see *Figure 14*). G1 collects three checks, and each member of the Successor Team signs a ten-year term note with a local bank for a conventional loan at the currently applicable interest rates. The T2 loans for G1(A) and G2(B) will probably *overlap* their T1 loans which should be expected to be paid off in about seven to eight years

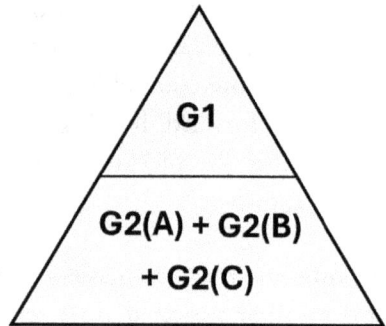

Figure 14

depending on current and anticipated growth rates and profitability levels.

When an individual purchases an Equity Interest in a Business, they may pay the purchase price with cash on hand, with proceeds from a bank loan, and/or with seller financed debt. If a seller agrees to accept a promissory note from a buyer for some or all of the purchase price (i.e., Seller Financing), the note payments may be structured in any number of ways. The two most common structures in succession planning purchases are fixed payment notes and profit-based notes.

Under both structures, the purchase price is agreed upon in advance and does not vary. Stock has a *strike price* on the day it is sold, even in a privately held Business, and that price is often tied to the FMV of that Business as determined by an Appraiser; it does not change after the sale regardless of business performance. Accordingly, earn-out arrangements are inappropriate as a payment device for an Equity purchase or sale.

With a commonly used fixed payment note, a buyer makes equal installment payments to the seller, with interest, over a set period (the "term"). Additional possibilities are explored in Lesson No. 32, *Seller Financing vs. Bank Financing.* A Profit-Based Note (see *Figure 15*), on the other hand, allows each payment to vary because it is equal to a certain percentage, as defined in the Note, of each quarterly gross profit distribution the buyer receives from the Business during the term. A Profit-Based Promissory Note must have a defined term, and if there is an outstanding balance on the Note at the end of the term, the buyer will be required to make a final lump sum payment to the seller, unless the seller agrees to extend the Note. At the very least, this payment format results in highly motivated buyers *and* sellers.

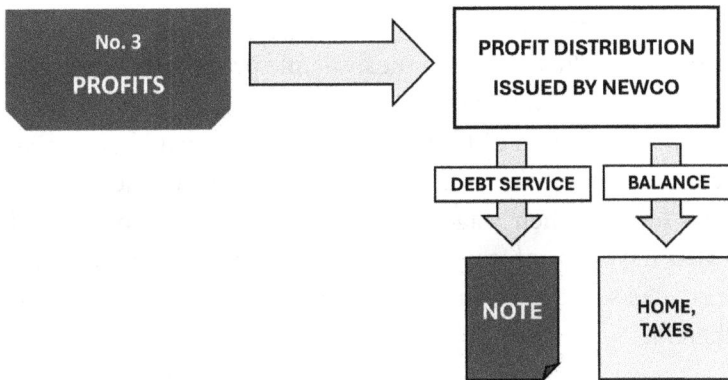

Figure 15

Even for G2 owners who obtain a conventional bank loan, it still can make sense to develop a spreadsheet model that uses a Profit-Based

Note format. Obviously, banks do not offer this repayment method, but this is still an effective way to think through the math especially when the successive Tranches are expected to overlap each other (i.e., when a second Tranche begins before the first Tranche has been fully paid off). A Profit-Based Note models each G2's pro rata share of profits from the acquired Equity in a specific Tranche. As an example, if G2(A) acquires 10% of G1's Equity in T1, then the modeling process looks only to G2(A)'s 10% pro rata share of Basket No. 3, or profits. While that much is obvious, the point is made clearer when, in T2, G2(A) buys another 10% of G1's Equity. In T2, the cash flow modeling focuses only on the 10% interest just acquired and only on the additional 10% pro rata share of profit distributions flowing to G2(A) to service that specific debt obligation. Each purchase is expected to stand on its own when being, effectively, serviced by the associated profit distribution dollars, which makes overlapping Tranches cash flow.

A good starting point, again for modeling purposes only, is to use only G2(A)'s after-tax profit dollars, assuming that G2(A)'s Basket No. 2 wage/compensation dollars are already spoken for—and they usually are. The profit dollars alone need to be able to service the debt on a pro forma spreadsheet, anticipating a strong but still conservative rate of top-line growth. In addition, we typically limit the profit-based debt service to 70% to 85% of the available profit distribution dollars in order to see the Note paid off in seven to eight years. A *cushion* is built in, just in case, and G2(A) is made aware that they can always devote more or all of the profit distribution dollars to the debt service, and even some of their wages or savings if they so choose. This basic math also serves to inform the discussions on price (vs. value) given the Business's success, or struggles, and G2(A)'s financial strength, or lack thereof.

To help illustrate the math and the timetable in our example, let's say that G1 decides to sell the rest of their Equity in year ten to the existing Successor Team—this will be T3. G1 will cash out in full at the then current FMV and the Successor Team owners will take out a third and final round of conventional bank financing, or possibly even an SBA-backed loan that could be used to refinance any remaining balance on the T2 purchases/sales. SBA loans, preferred by lenders involving intangible asset business models, can only be used in a Succession Plan when G1 sells all of their Equity. The loan will again likely be amortized for up to 10 years, even though the math suggests that the loans can each be paid for more quickly as long as the Business continues to grow and prosper which, by T3, should be completely *on the shoulders* of the Successor Team. This is how, and why, a ten-year Succession Plan for G1 equals something closer to a fifteen to twenty-year Plan for G2s and G3s.

As each Tranche is paid for, servicing the debt for each succeeding Tranche tends to become easier and the amortization process tends to become shorter, or condensed, which is good because the price of the Equity, hopefully from G1's perspective, will have grown significantly. In effect, there is an acceleration curve over the course of several Tranches. As an example, consider that G2(A) finishes paying off T1 and now has 20% of the profit dollars from Basket No. 3 to finish paying off the additional 10% equity purchase in T2. The Profit-Based Note approach isolates each purchase for modeling and planning purposes because of the tendency to overlap the equity buy-ins, but nothing stops G2(A) from accelerating the process and retiring their debt sooner if the cash flow is there. Of course G1 is watching. This part of the math also makes the underwriting process at a lending bank more palatable.

Key takeaways up to this point with regard to making the math work:

- T1 is the hardest part of a Succession Plan—worst case, seller financing can make the math work out

- Profitability and growth directly impact the value of a Business, as well as how investable it is

- Price tends to lag value in a Professional Services Business, sometimes by a little and sometimes by a lot—start with a formal business appraisal every time and figure it out from there

It is wise to also consider, with the help of a good legal draftsperson, adding in some formulaic safeguards on the debt service in the event of a material downturn in a Business's revenue stream. Such provisions can be included or added to the Buy-Sell Agreement and/or the promissory notes and may provide for a reduction in payments if the Business has been hindered in such a way that it is long term and, perhaps, permanent. One example is that growth or profits substantially fail to meet expectations, leaving the investors with no practical way to extinguish the debt. Banks don't care and that isn't their business model. Sellers who act as the bank (i.e., Seller Financing) will care and that matters in the early Tranches of a Succession Plan.

Common mistakes that founders make in T1 is to start too late and then move too slow, which changes the math, and the results in many cases. Some first time owners and sellers gravitate to a do-it-yourself Plan where they sell just 1% or 2% at a time, every year for ten years, for example. The thinking goes that the small buy-ins are easier for the G2 owner(s) to handle and finance, and if things don't work out, the remaining sales can simply be canceled. Kind of a no harm, no foul method. I accept the theory, but I've never seen it actually work.

The problem with this *inch-by-inch approach* is that next generation owners don't get very excited about a 1% to 2% equity interest; it just isn't very motivational. Second, each sale of Equity should be preceded by a formal appraisal given that this may be a highly regulated Professional Service, and it is restricted stock under state Blue Sky Rules. Appraisals can be time consuming and expensive (the only way around this is a series of seller financed transactions and guessing at the value of a Business allows for a buyer's opinion as well). Third, in a fast growing Business, the slow, incremental approach is more expensive over time. Finally, a 1% to 5% owner is not a reliable continuity partner in a Buy-Sell Agreement. There is simply no career length commitment in this approach until, probably, the eighth, ninth or tenth buy-in. That's a long time to wait to see if your next generation owners have what it takes.

At some point, in every Succession Plan, you just have to do the math.

LESSON NO. 22:
NO BOOK BUILDING
ALLOWED! (IN A BUSINESS)

Many Professional Service Practices (using the latter word as specifically defined in Lesson No. 2) tend to utilize a common, simple starting point for newer, younger associates called Book building. Basically, in a Practice model where clients are the medium of value, as opposed to Equity, the goal of an incoming associate or contractor is to "go get more clients!" Many, if not most next generation professionals don't survive this process beyond the first few years, and that's the point. Those who are good at getting a client base established are the "keepers." Practices are the testing grounds.

Practice owners are often reluctant to add a non-proven revenue producer to the payroll, not wanting to take the risk of one or more failed hires and the payroll commitment. My observation is that this is a lose/lose proposition for the founding owner(s). If the founder is right and their new revenue producer fails, out they go and you try again with someone else. But if they surprise you and end up succeeding, those Book owners are just as likely to walk away and take their clients with them. Either way, the Practice owner is out of pocket for the cost and time invested.

Accounting, law, independent financial services or insurance-based Practices, just to name a few of the Professional Services, are typically operated under a single trade name or DBA. From a single leased office space that presents a single identity to the public, a Practice is often supported by one or more (sometimes many) individuals within each location who are building their own Books. The Book builders/owners share office space, a receptionist, a phone and computer system with the Practice owner; they may even share revenue, but they do not share clients other than some joint case work.

The problem is, building separate Books can undermine the entire Business building process. Those individuals own their Books and any value associated with it. There is no singular, business value for a *group* of Book builders. As a Practice grows into a Business, individual, internal Book building must end. I realize that there are many different Professional Service venues, or occupations, and this may not be a universal problem. If this isn't an issue for you, please proceed to the next Lesson. If there is even a chance that your next generation PSPs might be thinking that they own the clients they serve and could walk across the street and take those clients elsewhere, please read on. You are not alone and we're talking about this for a reason.

The good news is that this issue may present a great opportunity. Professional Services typically engender many Book builders. Businesses that want to implement a Succession Plan need younger, experienced owners who know how to generate revenue and service clients. Book owners often have something to trade, which gives them a ticket into a Business and an Equity Interest.

One of the biggest challenges to implementing a Succession Plan is finding the necessary talent to work hard and make the monetary investment. Where do you find those people? I'd argue that they're all around you, at least in the Professional Service venues I'm familiar with. There are typically more Book builders and owners, i.e., sole proprietorships, than Practice and Business owners combined. A twenty or thirty-something year old Book owner can agree to join your Business via a Tax-Neutral Exchange and become an equity owner without having to buy in initially and take on debt service, if the Business sets up the appropriate entity (see Lesson Nos. 12 and

14). The smaller Practice models are effectively training the needed talent and may not offer any way up *the ladder of success*, at least in terms of Equity ownership. A growing, profitable, valuable Business can be the perfect answer—as long as the Business leadership doesn't fall into the Book building trap.

My advice is to cultivate two streams of talent for probable future ownership. One is the tried and tested method of hiring, training and rewarding home grown labor. Put these folks on the payroll and nurture them. If you have a G2 already, let that next generation owner share the process and the Business culture with your younger, newer team members. I'd involve G2 in the process as early as the first interview of a new prospect. Share the culture of ownership and business perpetuation.

The other way is to cultivate established Book builders. Most Book owners operate as sole proprietors which means that they operate a two-basket cash flow system (overhead expenses in one basket, and wages/profits combined in the second basket) and they may not intuitively understand the benefits of being a minority owner. Share the concept of Shareholder Value (see Lesson No. 9) and how your well-structured Business can help a Book owner build greater wealth over time as a member of the Successor Team.

Do both. These two streams of talent should support a long-term Succession Plan.

LESSON NO. 23:
LEARNING TO BE A GOOD
STEWARD OF OWNERSHIP

A properly structured business can theoretically last forever, or certainly well beyond the founding owner's career. The concept of being a good steward of ownership is that founding owners can use their businesses to accomplish good and to take care of *all* its stakeholders—clients, owners, employees, and the surrounding community. A well-managed business and purposeful leadership are agents of positive change.

Starting at a very basic level, being an equity steward is about setting up a business's documentation to support a culture of continuity—specifically addressing when and how founding owners must offer to sell their equity at specific, predetermined intervals. This functionality supports next generation investment and long-term involvement in the business. As an overarching philosophy, stewardship emphasizes that owning equity comes with responsibilities beyond, or at least in addition to, profit and value maximization. Blending the short-term goals of a business with the long-term goals of the stakeholders is how one becomes a good steward of ownership.

Many successful family businesses have been built on a foundation of long-term stewardship, with owners prioritizing the generational health and sustainability of the business over short-term gains. There is absolutely no reason, however, that family-like businesses and professional service businesses with unrelated owners or leaders cannot do the same. Equity stewardship in a private business is an important philosophy that supports a powerful set of tools to reshape today's business landscape and includes:

1. **Attracting and Retaining Talent**: In a competitive job market, employees are increasingly seeking ownership opportunity and a stake in the businesses they work for. Equity stewardship allows private businesses to attract and retain top talent by offering them a share of the company's success.

2. **Alignment of Interests:** Equity stewardship aligns the interests of employees with those of the business owners. When employees have a financial stake in the company, they are more likely to be invested in its long-term growth and profitability.

3. **Motivation and Productivity:** Equity can be a powerful motivator for key employees. Knowing that their efforts directly contribute to the value of their stake in the company can boost morale, engagement, and productivity.

4. **Succession Planning:** Equity stewardship can be an effective tool used through a formal Succession Plan in a privately held, Professional Services Business. By gradually transferring ownership to key employees, business owners can ensure a smooth transition and continuity of leadership.

5. **Tax Advantages:** Depending on the specific plan design, equity stewardship can offer tax advantages for the business and its owners.

6. **Increased Business Value:** Companies with strong equity stewardship programs tend to have higher employee retention, productivity, and overall business value. This can make the business more attractive to potential investors (G2s and G3s) or acquirers.

...and that is the short list. Going back to basics and supporting the more practical purposes of this book, being a good steward of ownership starts with documenting your Business's specific set of rules to address when and how owners might step out of the *Equity circle* and voluntarily relinquish their ownership interest. Every owner, for instance, wants to be able to sell their Equity Interest, someday, at current Fair Market Value (FMV), for cash, at long-term capital gains rates. Accordingly, being a good steward of ownership requires prospective sellers who want to sell their Equity under these circumstances to adhere to certain, written, pre-established guidelines if they want their full expectations to be met.

Functionally, the Business owners can agree as a group that in order to meet a seller's reasonable expectations when selling Equity, there will be established and reasonable expectations in return from the remaining owners. A common requirement is that a seller must give at least 24 months of notice to obtain their full benefits. In the event an owner leaves and wants to sell their equity on just two weeks' notice, then the FMV of their Equity Interest may be discounted and payment terms may be applied through Seller Financing rather than a lump sum through bank financing. These **Stewardship Rules** are put in place to ensure the Business remains liquid and sustainable, and that the Business has time to address the loss of talent. These rules tend to go further and be more proactive than those in a typical Buy-Sell Agreement.

Stewardship Rules, might even include a requirement that G1(s) cannot hold more than 50% of the Equity Interests in the Business at age 60, and no more than 25% of the Equity Interests by age 65, and must sell, or offer to sell, all of their Equity by age 70—adjust the numbers and ages for your situation. The idea is that *putting stock into play* at set, predetermined intervals helps to ensure that the next generation plans for, and can make, the necessary Equity investments during their careers.

These Stewardship Rules, along with all the buy-sell provisions, should be reviewed every couple of years by all the owners, especially as the Business grows in value and the owners of significant amounts of Equity get older. It also is better to document all this from the outset, while everyone is getting along well and are focused on the future and all the opportunities it may bring. In time, Stewardship Rules become a part of a Business's culture of sustainability.

LESSON NO. 24:
GOVERNANCE: INSTALLING
A BOARD OF DIRECTORS

A Book or a Practice, as we defined the terms back in Lesson No. 2, are for all practical purposes, *forces of one*. Guided by a single owner, the decision chain is short, quick, and often without recourse—there's nobody to blame but yourself if you make the wrong decision. The dynamics change when a Business has four or five minority owners, as in a 65%/20%/10%/5% ownership structure. How do decisions get made? Who makes the decisions? Do the smaller, younger owners even have a voice? Your investors will want to know these answers up front.

Practically, small businesses need to move fairly quickly and efficiently to compete and to get things done. Listening to everyone's ideas is usually a good thing; making decisions and moving ideas forward is quite another. In this vein, many founders choose to install a Board or Directors, often called the Managers in an LLC, to oversee more important decisions and to create a formal governance structure for the larger owners and more senior decision makers.

Let's set the table for this Lesson. Newco, LLC, taxed as either a Partnership or an S-Corporation, or both (see the Hybrid Entity Structure in Lesson No. 14) is set up with a single-class of equity, and 1,000,000 shares are authorized and issued. Business value based on a recent appraisal is $2,100,000 (or $2.1M). All of these shares are or should be fully vested and fully voting. Following Tranche One, or T1, the ownership structure is, in this example, 75%/20%/5%, G1/G2/G3, respectively. To enhance the picture, G1 is 61 years old and wants to work until age 70, G2 is 45 years old, and G3 is 28 years old.

To state the obvious, in any vote of shares, G1 wins! But that doesn't work very well for owners like G2 in this example. G2, who agreed with G1 on a buy-in price of $375,000 at the time of the Equity purchase, obtained a personal guaranteed, ten-year amortized, conventional bank loan. G2 wants and needs some control over their significant investment and the Business building and growth processes to come. The solution is to make both G1 and G2 Directors on the Board.

At the Director level, voting is handled in a different way than voting shares of stock. In simplest terms, it is one vote per Director regardless of how much Equity each Director might own, now or in the future. In Newco's Operating Agreement, the Managers, or Directors as we'll call them, are each empowered to vote on a set list of key decisions for the Business that often include the following:

- Selling the Business to an outside buyer
- Entering into a long-term lease agreement
- Taking on a debt obligation greater than $XX.XX
- Adding a new owner
- Diluting ownership by onboarding an owner
- Adding a second class of stock
- Merging into someone else's business

...and those are just for starters. Your list may well be much longer. On these specific issues, the two Directors each have one vote regardless of how much Equity they own which means that they must reach a consensus to move forward on these issues. Of course, this list can and should be adjusted over time as the Business evolves, providing both Directors agree. In sum, this governance provision ensures that partners act like partners and leave their stock certificates at home.

As a good rule of thumb, new Directors are added to the Board if and when they own about 20% of the total authorized and issued stock or Equity of the Business. This is not a rule of law, but my experience suggests that it is a good rule to abide by. The 5% owner, in contrast, has the ability to influence but not to control and will not be a Director unless and until they acquire and pay for a larger Equity Interest.

As your Business grows in value and size and your Succession Plan evolves, you have some additional tools to use when considering adding Director Nos. 3 and 4. In Newco, LLC's Operating Agreement, you (with the help of a good business attorney) can have two different lists, for example. On one list are the key decisions listed above for which a consensus of all Directors is required. On a second list of slightly less critical issues, two out of three or a majority of the Directors might be adequate, assuming the Board has more than two Directors in the future. It's your Business and your Operating Agreement and with a little foresight and some imagination, you can set up a governance structure that fits your needs and preferences.

That said, installing a Board of Directors is best done early when the founding owner or owners can create the supporting bedrock for this valuable, profitable, investable, growing and sustainable business through a short, efficient decision-making chain. The younger next generation owners will learn what they're investing in and how the governance and voting works via their due diligence efforts and they can then decide for themselves. G1 might even enshrine themself as the Chairperson of the Board and take on the additional duties of representing the Board outside of its meetings, running the Board meetings and issuing the agenda, and ensuring that the other Directors work as a unit.

Finally, think about the long-term functionality of the Board and the "one person, one vote" rule in the context of an evolving Succession

Plan. In your Plan, it may well be necessary and appropriate at some point for you to individually sell Equity until you own less than 50%. By having a permanent seat on the Board, you can retire on-the-job or at your own pace, absent stewardship rules, and still have a meaningful voice in the Business operations. In the case where there is more than one G1, a Board seat for each founder also makes it easier for two or three G1's to own unequal amounts of Equity, but still have an equal voice in the governance of the Business.

This is all part of building with the end in mind. In my experience, it comes sooner than you think.

LESSON NO. 25:
THE CONTROL MECHANISMS
OF A SMALL BUSINESS

One of the greatest joys of my life was graduating from law school, passing the bar and starting my career as an attorney *and an owner*. I eschewed the law firm associate role for a host of reasons, but I'd always really wanted to be a sole proprietor, a force of one!

As the sole owner, I did everything that needed doing until I hired some much needed help. Providing legal support, writing documents, crafting a haphazard marketing plan, maintaining the books, paying the bills—the weeks were long, but I had my hands on every aspect of my own Book. I felt totally in control, and I was—of everything. I liked it that way, until one day, as I gathered more clients, I ran out of time—literally, there were simply no more hours available in a given week. I needed help, and I needed to learn to delegate authority and responsibility. To be certain, they don't teach that in law school.

Years later, as my Book grew into a stronger, larger Practice, I was not only the owner, I knew more about the law than anyone else in my small office. I liked it that way! In my Business, however, I learned that it was not a good thing—I had to learn to hire people that were better than me or could grow to be better than me in one or more specific roles. Slowly loosening the reins of control is harder than it sounds and many founders simply surround themselves with lesser talent, whether by design or default.

After seven or eight years into the Business building process, after we hired a skilled, experienced Marketing Director, I first learned what an annual, detailed marketing plan and budget actually looked like. More importantly, I realized how much I didn't know about that specific line of work. And why would I? I had no formal training in the marketing functions, like most PSPs, probably. The same held true when we brought in a full-time Bookkeeper, a full-time Cash Flow Analyst (a CFA®), a full-time Sales Manager, and so on. I learned to set my ego aside and hire people better than me, and we got better, and bigger, and stronger, even as I did less and made fewer decisions. I had to *let go* to succeed and build a Business. I learned that I couldn't and didn't need to control everything to be successful, but I still wanted to have control over the Business.

The message in this Lesson is that you can and should let go of much of the work and still maintain control over the direction of your Business if you understand the mechanics of the process. Maintaining control over a Business with other owners, multiple generations of leadership, and key employees is an intricate process in a growing and valuable enterprise. In most Professional Service Businesses, there are as many as four distinct levels of command and control that can be utilized or coordinated to protect your interests:

- Officers
- Directors
- Shareholders
- Key Employees

As illustrated, understand that control flows downward from the top (Shareholders) to the bottom (Key Employees). Meanwhile, accountability flows upward, with Officers accountable to the Board of Directors, and the Board of Directors accountable to the Shareholders (see *Figure 16*).

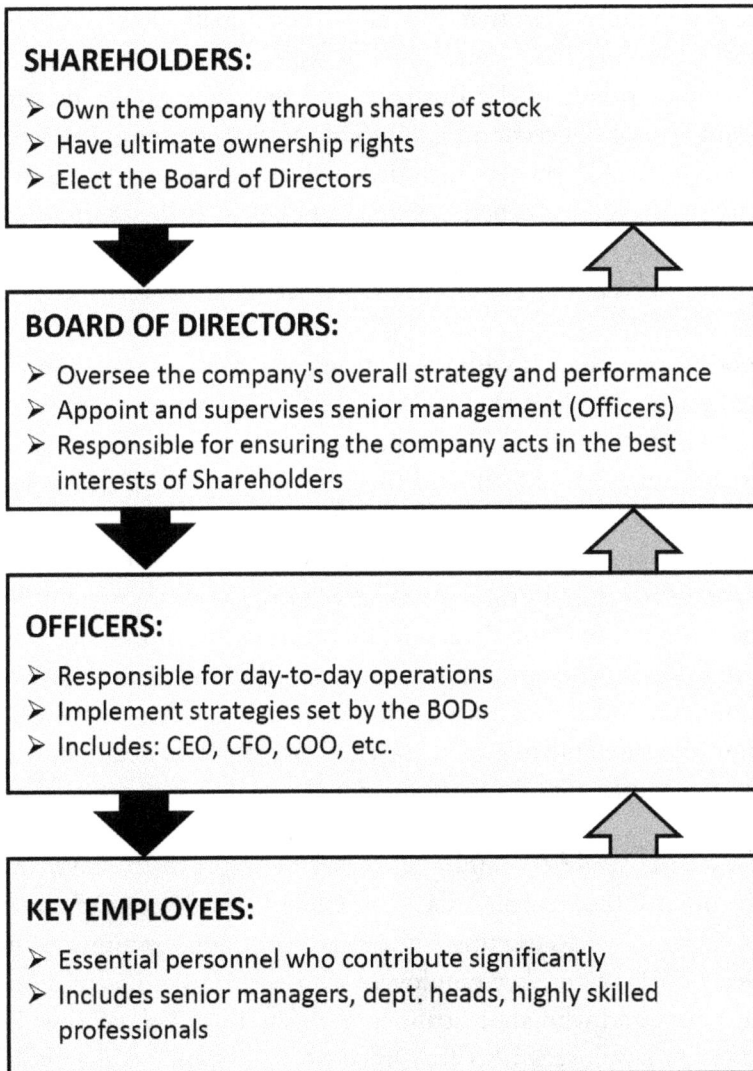

SHAREHOLDERS:

➤ Own the company through shares of stock
➤ Have ultimate ownership rights
➤ Elect the Board of Directors

BOARD OF DIRECTORS:

➤ Oversee the company's overall strategy and performance
➤ Appoint and supervises senior management (Officers)
➤ Responsible for ensuring the company acts in the best interests of Shareholders

OFFICERS:

➤ Responsible for day-to-day operations
➤ Implement strategies set by the BODs
➤ Includes: CEO, CFO, COO, etc.

KEY EMPLOYEES:

➤ Essential personnel who contribute significantly
➤ Includes senior managers, dept. heads, highly skilled professionals

Figure16

If control is an issue at the G1 level, and it usually is, then the founder should hold on to 51% of the outstanding shares, or Equity, for as long as possible. That's really the starting point for most first generation senior owners, or G1s as the Business grows around them. But there is more to it than that. Shareholders of small, closely held businesses rarely vote their shares on key issues. In fact, most decisions are made by others in the Business, and they may not be owners at all. And as your Succession Plan unfolds over time, it is quite possible that everyone, G1 owners included, will own less than 51% of the Equity. However and whenever that happens, it helps to understand well in advance how the control mechanisms work and which aspects you really need to exert control or to actually maintain legal control.

A good place to start is with the Officers of a Business such as a CEO (Chief Executive Officer), a COO (Chief Operations Office), a CFO (Chief Financial Officer). The point is that these leaders have specific roles and duties to perform and their salaries are tied to their specific functions and talents. Day-to-day, Officers make almost all the meaningful decisions that move a Business forward and help it grow and prosper. Officers in a Professional Services Business are usually shareholders as well, but not always. More information is provided on the role of Officers, and specifically that of a CEO, in Lesson No. 29. As the founder, and right after securing your desired level of ownership, assume the title and role of the CEO—as your Business grows, you may need a different CEO at some point, but that is an issue for later.

Experienced, loyal key employees may be charged with one or more of the other Officer roles. A CCO or Chief Compliance Officer, even a CMO or Chief Marketing Officer, are common examples of non-owner, non-Director, key employees who wield a significant amount of authority and who are instrumental in the Business's success. Even though key employees who are Officers have no votes as shareholders or Directors, they have an enormous amount of influence over the Business and they all report to the CEO.

A Director who serves on the Board (covered in the previous Lesson) is almost always a shareholder who owns and has made a significant investment in the Business. To be clear, Directors do not have to be owners; in fact, outsiders to the Business can play a significant role on the Board in a limited or advisory capacity. Directors who are shareholders will each have one vote on a written list of principal issues reserved for the Directors to approve or not and regardless of how much equity they own in the Business. Directors report to the shareholders, and they direct the Officers, who direct the key employees, who direct the staff members.

Shareholders are, of course, the owners, but they are also usually the Officers and the Directors. And that is why we're talking about the control mechanisms of a small business, a Professional Services Business specifically. G1s who worry about control have a couple of powerful advantages. One, they often work full time (and then some) and know more about the day-to-day operations than anyone else. Two, the G1 owners have more experience, and three, are the majority owners (individually or cumulatively). Being there every day in the business effectively gives them full and complete control. But in time that will change; it must change for a Succession Plan to work and that is where the intricacies of the control mechanisms get more interesting.

The need for and application of these distinct levels of control starts to make more sense when the ownership structure evolves to something like 30%/30%/20%/10%/10% among five owners and at least two generations of ownership. As the G1 ownership level starts to get older and begins to throttle-back in terms of time in the office and hours worked, the growth and profitability of the Business will demand daily, proficient decision makers. At two or three days a week, on average, a founding owner can retain their minority shareholder status and votes, a role as a Director with one vote regardless of equity holdings, perhaps the role of Chairman of the Board, and…that's it. That is the evolution of control in a growing, investable, valuable, sustainable Business.

Let's circle back to the role of shareholder and add one important caveat. If one of the founders, a G1, insists on retaining a 51% interest or more until their full retirement, there may be a real problem. In a smaller, $2.0M valued Business, the Successor Team can likely step up and take over and bank finance G1's entire Equity Interest fairly easily and safely. But in a Business valued at $10.0M or more, buying out and cashing out a 60% G1 owner on short notice may prove nearly impossible, or is simply too great a risk for a small Successor Team. The best ways to address such issues are to apply the proper stewardship rules covered previously, or to agree through the Buy-Sell Agreement to substantially discount G1's interest or to require use of Seller Financing over an extended period (15 years, perhaps) at minimal interest rates. Absent such remedies and concessions, G1's position may imperil the Succession Plan and render the Business uninvestable.

To close out this Lesson, my personal advice to the G1's out there—hold on to 51% ownership for as long as you can, but not forever and not past age 65. At some point, the Business has to move beyond the one dominant shareholder model to support a Succession Plan. Set your Business up from the outset with a Board of Directors and give yourself a permanent seat, maybe even after your retirement. If you can't, or won't, then be honest with your Successor Team and set the Business up for an Exit Plan. You don't need investors, you need a buyer. And sometimes that is how the story ends.

INTERMISSION

"Pause you who read this, and think for a moment…" wrote Charles Dickens a long time ago, and that is good advice. At the half-way point in this book, a few reminders, highlights, previews, and course adjustments:

1. Capitalized terms are those defined in this book and captured in the Glossary. Such terms are used specifically, not generically unless, of course, they are just ordinary proper nouns! There is an extensive Glossary in this book which underscores the point that a Succession Plan relies upon some unique and specific terminology.

2. There are 50 Lessons in this book and you are half-way through. Aren't you glad there aren't a hundred Lessons?! Well, maybe there are, but you best learn the other 50 Lessons in the course of your own Succession Plan. We'll add more Lessons as well as illustrations based on your thoughts, needs and concerns—so please tell me what you're thinking, what I might have missed, and how I can help at:

www.DavidGrauSr.com

There is no cost to ask questions, schedule a one-on-one call, to learn and enjoy the blog posts, new lessons, illustrations and more. I hope you'll visit and share your story.

3. Not every Professional Services owner should have, or needs, a Succession Plan. Depending on your circumstances, selling what you've built to a third party or an outside buyer may indeed be the better choice. Maybe you have a true family business and simply want to adapt a few of the Lessons to fit your needs and improve your current plan. The best way to know for sure? Design and model a Plan, or at least have a thorough understanding of what the term means and the possibilities at hand and make a fully informed decision. In the end, what's right for you is what's right.

4. One of the unusual benefits of a Succession Plan is that it slows... things... down..., often a benefit to both the founders (G1s) and the successors (G2s and G3s). The weight of buying Equity after taxes, incrementally as it grows in value, using bank loans at then current interest rates, is a bit like buying a house. Younger owners can get a lot more house, if that is the goal, with a twenty-year mortgage than a five-year mortgage; a Succession Plan similarly extends the amortization period using multiple Tranches with multiple Equity sales and purchases. Most G1 owners gravitate towards the idea of working less hard for a longer period. G1s want to see a return on their long-term investment too, and most enjoy the work that they do, at least more days than not. Slowing the process and/or extending the timeframe over which the transition is completed can be a good thing for both sides.

5. As your guide, I cannot overemphasize the importance of being good stewards of ownership. Every founder must determine with their Successor Team what that means to them, but it should be carefully considered, applied, and considered again. Ownership of a small business, especially in the Professional Services world where the next client to walk through the door could be the last, is a special thing. It

should be treated accordingly by each generation and each generation needs to respect those who came before, and those who will come after. Be fair. Be honest. Take what you've earned, not what you deserve, and teach all who follow to do the same.

6. Though there is no rule of law on this issue, experience and observation dictate that at 20% Equity ownership, banks/lenders start to consider that to be the level where a personal guarantee on Business debt comes into play—think of a Business Line of Credit or other loans to the Business. That's been a fairly consistent number across the country and from bank-to-bank in our succession planning work. Be aware of this even though a 20% owner is still in a minority position. In fact, this is what guides our general recommendation that next generation owners be awarded a Board seat at about a 20% Equity Interest level.

7. I wrote the first draft of my first book on this subject matter for the financial services world (investment advisors, broker-dealers, money managers, and insurance professionals) in 2013. At the time, I owned a small house perched on a cliff overlooking a rocky coast line and the vast Pacific Ocean. A hundred yards to the north was a small, working harbor. As I struggled for the words to describe the business building challenges in those fields of endeavor, I came up with the idea of using the vessels I saw out my window.

The story I told in greater detail in that book, and since in hundreds of speaking events, equated life rafts (or the Zodiac's zipping around the shallows in search of whales) with Book owners, or sole proprietorships. Ocean-going ships resembled, to me, a strong, durable Business. I argued that a group of life rafts lashed together, the most common "business building" scenario twenty years ago in that space was not like a ship. It was not a business at all, no matter how many Book owners there were.

And it worked—complex dynamics made simple. In fact,

this is where the "onboarding" term came from as a life raft owner could, figuratively speaking, paddle up to a ship and offer to exchange their small treasure for some Equity and a permanent place on a bigger, safer, more durable vessel. How this story applies to the many diverse types of Professional Services remains to be seen.

8. There are many, many types of Professional Services and each one has a competitive level of profitability that is appropriate for and tied to the cost of the delivery of those specific services. A veterinary clinic, for instance, might have a third to a half of the profits of an independent money manager or financial advisor—and while several Lessons used the figure of 25% as an example of strong profitability, what's normal to your profession is what your Plan can be designed to work with. I'd still argue that managing or balancing owners' comp with profits is a smart way to adjust that bottom-line number, but that only works for the equity owners. Each Succession Plan and every different Professional Service model requires that you *do the math*... maybe with a little help. In most cases, there is an answer to be had.

LESSON NO. 26:
THE RESIDUAL EQUITY STRATEGY

In most Plans, G1 gradually sells their Equity, Tranche-by-Tranche, down to 0.0% ownership at some point. The Successor Team of G2s and, one day, G3s, are tasked with gradually buying all of G1's Equity even as, especially as, the value and price of the shares grow. The Equity acquisitions are after-tax and, using a conventional bank loan, with interest. Collectively, this is a very heavy lift as you've learned in the preceding Lessons. And with fewer members of the Successor Team in some instances, the buy-in process can indeed seem overwhelming.

The Residual Equity strategy we will examine in this Lesson offers a possible solution, and it provides benefits to both generations of ownership. The strategy lies in G1(s) holding on to some of their Equity into perpetuity, or for the remainder of their natural lives, at which point the Business redeems G1's remaining interest and cashes out their estate at FMV. In sum, as a G1, you don't have to sell all your Equity in the course of your career and prior to your full retirement; as a G2, you don't have to buy out all the founder's Equity, at least not within the typical retirement time horizon. Residual Equity can change the rules in a meaningful way.

A typical Residual Equity strategy might allow G1 to continue to own up to 10% to 20% of the issued and outstanding shares of the Business, and to continue to benefit from the associated profit distributions and stock appreciation rights. Conversely, G2 does not have to worry about buying and financing all of G1's stock, especially if they're still paying off a loan on the previous Tranche(s). As the Business's entire client base tacitly observes the Business Succession Plan unfolding and witnesses G1's gradual on-the-job retirement in favor of a younger Successor Team, it can be beneficial to tell the existing clients, and even prospective clients, that the founder is still an owner of the Business.

More likely than not, G1, once in the Residual Equity phase of the Succession Plan, will drop off the payroll, and may give up the proverbial corner office, or not. Some businesses find real value in providing an office to a senior member who is no longer an active producer or service provider. The value lies in having these senior owners and team members spend unpaid time in the office providing guidance and wisdom to the next generations of PSP's and owners. Residual Equity often helps G1 stay just enough involved to make retirement less of a sudden stop and to provide some long-term growth benefits and upside. This strategy can also be used to find the additional time that might be needed to onboard another member to the Successor Team to help buy out this last block of Equity.

In Lesson No. 23, we explored what it means to be a good steward of ownership. The process involves documenting the rules for how and when Equity must be relinquished by aging owners to provide the next generation in the Plan with an opportunity to buy in and to perpetuate the Business. A Residual Equity strategy works hand-in-hand with stewardship rules but serves to extend the timetable for when senior ownership must sell all of their remaining Equity. Residual Equity, of course, is a special case and should be considered as such in the overall stewardship rules. There are many other possibilities to consider such as wages, bonuses, a stipend for sitting on the Board, perhaps as a voting member or in an advisory capacity. Does G1 get an office? Health care coverage? Lots to consider in the modeling of this strategy. Sometimes these options can bridge the gap between two generations of ownership trying to work out the details of the final Tranche.

Some Professional Service Business models, if regulated and needing licensure to deliver the services, may not be allowed to have a residual owner unless that person retains licensure in all states where the Business has clients and, in most cases, E&O (Errors & Omissions insurance) or malpractice insurance coverage. Sometimes these costs are material and sometimes not. The financial services world where I come from, for instance, has regulatory provisions that would not allow a non-licensed individual to share in a Business's profit distribution dollars once they relinquish licensure; there is no issue with a non-licensed owner remaining on the payroll. This is something to keep in mind given your Professional Services venue and to perform due diligence on.

Finally, many of the clients I have consulted with to design and implement a Succession Plan start too late, or a little late, as mentioned in a recent Lesson. In fact, starting late is more the norm than not! I'm not piling on here. The point is that a shortened timetable can be rectified by using a Residual Equity strategy. Suddenly, the Business and the next generation owners have an extra five to ten years, perhaps, to work with and G1 has some additional upside and a way to stay involved even if limited to cheering on the team from the near sidelines.

LESSON NO. 27: MAINTAINING ADEQUATE LIQUIDITY IN A FLOW-THROUGH ENTITY STRUCTURE

One of the common themes in this book is the need for a high (or higher) level of profitability to support the succession planning process. In our Three-Basket Cash Flow System, Basket No. 3 reflects the results of the profit generating strategy in a growing Business. In addition, the entity structures we've explored and generally recommended, depending on your specific fact pattern and goals, are all Tax Conduits or flow-through entities which are designed to send those Basket No. 3 profit dollars home to the shareholders on a pro rata basis, in part to service the debt from Equity purchases by the members of the Successor Team. The point is that those profit dollars need to be paid out to the owners.

Let's start with a simple fact: growing Businesses need cash to operate safely and sustainably. Another fact is that, every so often, a recession hits and Businesses often struggle with growth and profitability even as expenses often increase against these economic headwinds. So how does a Professional Services Business maintain sufficient liquidity against unforeseen events, especially when the Successor Team needs its profit distribution checks to service debt and augment a fixed or flat wage structure (as you'll learn more about in Lesson No. 35!)?

The answer, just to be clear, relies on *the Business* to maintain a certain level of liquidity and not on the owners, or at least not on the younger owners who are simply not ready for this in T1. I experienced a cash call during the Great Recession in my own Business and I would not advocate that as a strategy for any owner of any age. Here is how we have taught larger, successful multi-owner Businesses in the past to manage the issue of business liquidity, conceding that there is more than this one way to address this issue.

Let's go back to *standing up* Newco, LLC, and filing or amending your Articles of Organization. Once the tax election is in place and the TIN/EIN has been issued to you, open up a primary checking account for Newco, but don't stop there. Also open up a Line of Credit (LOC) for the Business if possible. For discussion purposes, let's start with a LOC for a Business that grosses up to $2.0M, of $250,000, and acknowledge that your bank will probably require personal guarantees from any owner who owns 20% Equity or more in your Business.

Then, also open up a Money Market account *for Newco*—we're still working on the Business side of the ledger to be clear. Gradually deposit, for example, about $50,000 or so a year into the Money Market account until it equals the LOC ($250,000). At this point, three or four years later, the Business will have $500,000 in liquidity plus whatever balance is on hand in the checking account. During good times, as the Business is growing and prospering, this liquidity plan, once completed, will allow the owners to run the Business's cash flow *on a very lean setting*, meaning you may not feel the need to have operational expenses in the checking account for six months. Now, maybe 45 to 60 days of cash flow will be sufficient, with all remaining cash flowing home through the profit channel (Basket No. 3), pro rata once a quarter or as the Business leaders prefer.

One of the reasons why we recommend *backfilling* the Money Market account over time is the effect of those retained earnings on the owners of the Business. In an S-Corporation, or an LLC/Partnership or LLC/S-Corporation, all Tax Conduit structures, the annual savings in the Money Market account flow home to each owner's 1120-S or K-1 on a pro rata basis, even though no money was, or will be, physically received by the Equity owners. This means the owners will pay taxes on money they never received, which can be hard on the younger, newer owners who are also servicing debt from their Equity purchases. This is the concept of "Phantom Income" and this is one of the ways it happens. Still, Businesses need capital to grow and survive and if the liquidity isn't maintained by the Business, it has to be maintained by the owners. At the G1 level, this is common, and commonly accepted as founders are accustomed to doing whatever it takes. It is much harder to ensure that each newer and younger owner is setting aside enough cash on the home front to support an immediate and perhaps substantial cash call. It is not a practical plan in most cases.

When the reserves in the Money Market account are material enough, the account can and should be specifically addressed within the structure of the Business's Buy-Sell Agreement.

In the Intermission section following Lesson No. 25, and previously in this Lesson, I suggested that many banks look at a 20% Equity owner as substantial and expect them to step forward as a guarantor on a Business Line of Credit or other Business debt. Applying this rule to this liquidity resolution, your entity documentation might also, or instead, resort to a cash call approach, but only from owners of 20% Equity or more. Your Business should treat the cash infusion from each owner as a loan to the Business, memorialized with a formal promissory note and an interest component. When we conduct our G2 introductory sessions during the Succession Planning design and implementation phase, we refer to these as the "Opportunities & Obligations" calls. This is an example of an owner's obligations.

Part of this discussion is also about G1s and G2s learning how to work together to build a bigger, stronger Business and to sustain it in good times and bad. And part of this discussion is about helping each preceding generation learn how to teach the next generation to properly and professionally work through the tough times, and to prepare for the inevitable economic challenges that could cripple a lesser prepared Business. Multi-generational Businesses don't just fail because they cannot seamlessly hand off the baton between each leg of the event; sometimes people just underestimate what it takes to run a Business with a significant and growing appetite for cash—an oversight that only happens once.

LESSON NO. 28:
THE ROLE OF LIFE INSURANCE
IN A SUCCESSION PLAN

In every Professional Services Business with two or more owners, regardless of their ages, the amount of ownership, or whether all owners are of similar age and start as founders (G1s), or we have a G1 and a G2, there needs to be a Buy-Sell Agreement in place. If your choice is an S-Corporation, the Buy-Sell Agreement is often called a Shareholders Agreement. If you are using or will use an LLC, the buy-sell provisions are addressed through the Operating Agreement or separately in a Members Agreement.

Regardless of what the document is titled, a Buy-Sell Agreement helps to establish the rules for how all owners will sell their Equity at some point in time. Remember that the triggering events in a Buy-Sell Agreement include termination of employment (yes, minority owners can be fired), loss of licensure, death, and disability, among other things. Getting to the point of this Lesson, one of the more important aspects of a Buy-Sell Agreement, when a triggering event occurs, is the funding mechanism—life insurance is one of the funding solutions. Before delving into how insurance can specifically be used as part of the solution set, let's *reset the table* and get our thoughts in order for this Lesson, putting the role of life insurance into proper context.

All the owners of a Business enter into a written Buy-Sell Agreement obligating themselves, individually, or as a group, to step forward as a buyer, or buyers, or as a Business entity, to pay the FMV of an Equity Interest from an owner who leaves. Buy-Sell Agreements are commonly referred to as a *double-edged sword* because the terms apply to all owners as a possible seller or as a possible buyer. That said, in a Succession Plan with one G1 who is 58 years old and two G2's in their thirties, in an 80%/10%/10%, G1/G2(A)/G2(B) ownership structure, the impact is quite different depending on the owner's perspective.

If G2(A) suddenly leaves their employment and relinquish their Equity Interest, either the Business or G2(B) will buy the Equity and finance it with a bank loan—one or the other needs to function as the successor and/or buyer. But if something happens to G1, it is a vastly different challenge, and this is the purpose of this Lesson. Let's make it interesting and say that G2(A) has completed their first Tranche buy-in and has no remaining debt from T1; G2(B) just recently bought in and they still have 9 years remaining on their amortization schedule on a conventional bank loan after making no down payment on their initial Equity purchase. Let's put the business value at $4.0M.

In about five or six years, if all goes well, G1 will have an excellent solution set in place with at least the two G2 owners—though I'd encourage the group to close the gap as soon as possible, moving from a G1/G2 cumulative ownership structure of 80%/20% to closer to 60%/40%. Until then, G1 has several viable options, other than avoiding dangerous events! One such dangerous event to be avoided is being a 65-year-old G1 who thought they were a year or two from retirement, now needing to spend their retirement savings to buy back shares from G2(A) who has gone off to discover the Loch Ness monster.

G1 can and should maintain a Drag-Along or Bring-Along Right in the Newco, LLC, documentation process (covered in more depth in Lesson No. 33). This contractual element provides G1 with the unilateral right to sell the Business to an outside buyer of G1's choice, provided it is done in a commercially reasonable manner. As such,

G1 could sell to a third-party, or use his control position to name a third-party as his continuity partner for the next, perhaps, three to five years, giving the Successor Team time to prepare for a sudden, triggering event.

Please pardon the long and winding contextual road here. Another common approach is to fund the Buy-Sell Agreement with life insurance—usually term insurance. The amount of the insurance does not need to be equal to the value of the insured's Equity. In a fast-growing business that's not really practical for most small business owners. The point of the term life insurance isn't to completely extinguish the debt, only to defray the cost of the Equity purchase. If there is a single G1 and a single G2 owner, they may well utilize a cross-purchase arrangement where each owner purchases and holds (as the beneficiary) the term policy on the other owner's life. Application of the insurance proceeds are dictated by the Buy-Sell Agreement, which is a contract executed by the two owners.

In cases where there are three or more owners, as in our example above, it is more common to have the Business buy and pay for the life insurance policies on all owners, not deducting the premium costs (another example of how Phantom Income can be created), naming the Business itself as the beneficiary. Paying the premiums with post-tax dollars should make the death benefit tax free, while deducting the premium as an expense, by the company or the shareholder, likely makes the death benefit taxable. The proceeds of any triggered policy are then contractually handled through the Buy-Sell Agreement in which case the Business (Newco, LLC as we've been calling it) redeems the exiting owner's shares in full, effectively retiring the deceased owner's shares and putting those shares back into the authorized but unissued category, leaving the surviving owners holding all the authorized and issued shares. In the event the life insurance proceeds are not sufficient to extinguish the debt, Newco could use cash reserves, Seller Financing, or even bank financing to fund the balance.

Occasionally, I've seen Professional Service owners obtain a massive insurance policy, run the premium costs through the Business, and then use the amount of insurance to set a corresponding fixed value in the Buy-Sell Agreement. This works on paper, but the problem is that if G1 doesn't die and trigger the life insurance funding and still leaves the Business, the Business's cash flow may well be insufficient to service the debt on the stated/inflated value. Also, any bank lender will probably defer to a formal valuation prepared by a qualified appraiser as to the Business's Fair Market Value; the amount of the life insurance policy will hold little sway.

We occasionally run into a do-it-yourself Succession Plan that relies entirely on life insurance as the funding mechanism to pay for the Equity value relinquished by any owner. Literally, the death of an owner is the centerpiece of the Plan. It is not unusual for founders to say, "I'm going to work until the day I die." Somehow, I've never understood why anyone would want to be part of a Succession Plan that requires you to die to realize your value! There are better ways, but life insurance certainly plays a role in the process.

A closing thought on life insurance. The purpose of using life insurance to fund or partially fund a Succession Plan and Buy-Sell Agreement is not financial security for your family; that is a separate policy. The purpose here is to protect the Business and all of its stakeholders—its employees, customers, and other owners, in addition to your own Equity.

I've had the privilege of working with some very talented and experienced life insurance specialists. These professionals can offer some intricate strategies and life insurance products to solve Buy-Sell Agreement issues in ways that most of us don't even know enough to ask about. This may provide an answer for you so don't let this Lesson, which is based on the most commonly used approaches by other PSPs, limit your thinking. Ask the questions, do the listening, and then make your best decision. Life insurance should always be included in your Buy-Sell Agreement funding mechanism.

LESSON NO. 29:
YOUR NAME, CEO

For those of you who currently own a Practice, the process of building a Business designed from the ground up to be valuable, profitable, and sustainable is momentous—it changes everything over time. One of the more difficult changes to adjust to is that the founder(s) must gradually shift from being entrepreneur and the primary (or one of the primary) revenue producer(s) to, at some point, a CEO, with all the attendant responsibilities.

Businesses need a full-time leader.

What makes this process so challenging is that not every entrepreneur is cut out for this role. It is often not a natural and easy transition. Frankly, the skill set, the passion, the education may not be there. Sometimes, the best person to be CEO comes from the ranks of long tenured, key employees; sometimes this person is brought in from outside the Business. In my own journey from Book builder to Practice owner to building a Business with 65 people, I realized that I didn't want to be the CEO and I probably wouldn't have been very good at it. I was well educated, and no one knew more about the work we did than I. And I was also passionate about the Business. And still, all those things didn't add up to the role or skill set of a CEO. Law school, as I recall, didn't offer a single class to help me prepare for such a task!

The point is, there will come a time when a Business becomes large enough and complex enough that it needs a full-time leader—not a part time leader and a part time service provider. My experience is that when a Business's gross revenue surpasses $5.0 million/year, formal Officer roles and duties become inevitable and unavoidable. Fight the tide if you wish, but a growing and valuable Business demands a full-time, dedicated leader. There is no fixed rule, though maintaining sustainable and strong revenue growth rates, and competitiveness with similarly sized businesses are early indicators. Entrepreneurs who have grand visions and the wherewithal to take on and manage the role of CEO will gravitate to the position sooner than later. Ultimately, what works for you and your Business is the right answer at least in the short term.

In the past, when helping to install a Board of Directors on the stand-up of a new entity, I often provided counsel with the help of our legal team about the Officer functions as well. Our common advice is to include Officer titles and the related duties and responsibilities in the body of your initial Operating Agreement or Partnership Agreement, perhaps long before formally appointing and empowering each of these Officers. Think of this step a shifting the culture from individual service providers to a coordinated team of Business builders. Understand that it is not unusual for these Officers to also be revenue producers and service providers, except for the CEO at some point.

Here are the definitions we use to start the process, often memorialized in the Operating Agreement (or the Bylaws if the Business is organized as a corporation, or a Partnership Agreement if you prefer—it is your Business, after all), and understanding that these descriptors should be adapted to your situation, and your Business's needs and goals:

Chief Executive Officer ("CEO"). The CEO shall establish the goals of the Company, provide for the organizational mission and vision, grow the value of the Company and ensure financial success, be responsible for capital allocation, and implement strategies for meeting the Company goals and the overall vision. The

CEO shall meet with other Company officers to determine organizational policies and procedures, advise and present quarterly performance reports to the Directors, oversee future planning for operations, encourage innovation and a collaborative work environment, and analyze reports of the Company to inform decisions and maintain effectiveness. The CEO may sign certificates for shares of the Company, deeds, mortgages, bonds, contracts, or other instruments, except when the signing and execution thereof have been expressly delegated by the Board of Directors or by this Operating Agreement to some other officer or agent of the Company or are required by law to be otherwise signed or executed by some other officer or in some other manner.

Chief Operating Officer ("COO"). The COO shall be responsible for strategy implementation and daily operations management, shall focus on increasing profits and operational efficiency and quality, promote workers to management positions, maintain or reduce service delivery costs, implement safety protocols, work with administrative staff to collect, manage, and distribute material information, and supervise and control all the assets; monitor the Company's budget and financial statements, and manage the daily affairs of the Company. The COO shall work with the CEO to align and achieve the Company's goals. In the event of the death of the CEO or their inability to act, the Chief Operating Officer shall perform the duties of the CEO, except as may be limited by resolution of the Board of Directors, with all the powers and subject to all the restrictions upon the CEO. In sum, the COO is a senior level executive who translates strategy into actionable steps, makes prompt and necessary adjustments to the Company operations, and who ensures that the Company's day-to-day operations run properly.

Chief Financial Officer ("CFO"). The CFO shall have charge and custody of and be responsible for all funds and securities of the Company, receive and give receipts for moneys due and payable to the Company from any source whatsoever, and deposit all such monies in the name of the Company in banks, trust companies, or other depositories selected in accordance with the provisions of the Operating Agreement, and in general perform all the duties incident to the office of Chief Financial Officer and such other duties as from time to time may be assigned to them by the CEO or by the Directors. The CFO shall also be responsible for identifying and mitigating financial risks to the Company and shall manage relationships with lenders and provide them with accurate financial statements. If required by the Board of Directors, the Chief Financial Officer shall give a bond for the faithful discharge of their duties in such amount and with such surety or sureties as the Directors shall determine.

The goal of developing this Officer-based structure, led by the Business's CEO, COO, CFO, is to:

(a) Help owners understand that running a Business is about more than just revenue production

(b) Help each owner understand and respect what their partners are tasked to do on a daily basis

(c) Provide support for future ownership compensation planning

(d) Provide clear information to the staff members as to which leaders are responsible for certain tasks

(e) Support a governance structure that is practical and skill-based, not centered on who's the oldest or the biggest producer or largest shareholder.

Some businesses combine the roles early on—as long as the work gets done, and it works for you, do it. Another possibility is to gradually assign a specific Officer's duties to a key employee or younger owner to see how well they manage it. If all goes well, and once most of the duties under a particular Officer's title are being handled, formally designate that person as the appropriate Officer.

Finally, notice all the duties and responsibilities that each Officer performs and consider how this impacts the governance, voting and control of the Business itself. The daily work, tasks and decisions performed by the Officers as they fulfill their duties is not subject to a vote. Officers and key employees actually make most of the decisions needed to help a small Business grow and prosper, obviously with oversight by the Board and the shareholders.

There comes a time in most Businesses when the "entrepreneurial approach" no longer works well. This is another of the key differences between owning a Practice and owning a Business. It is a good problem to have.

LESSON NO. 30:
THE ISSUE OF "BASIS"

Basis is generally the amount of your capital investment in property for tax purposes. In most situations, the Basis of an asset is equal to what you paid for it, whether with cash, debt obligations, or other property. This Lesson will answer the questions of why it matters in the course of a Succession Plan and how the issue of Basis (also called Cost Basis) separately affects G1 owners and G2/G3 owners.

In a Succession Plan, Cost Basis matters because it is the starting point for calculating gain or loss on the purchase or sale of stock or Equity. If you sell an Equity interest in a Professional Services Business for more than its Cost Basis, you will realize a capital gain; if you sell equity for less than its Cost Basis, you will realize a loss. In certain situations where the Cost Basis can and has been depreciated, the amount between the original Basis and the depreciated Basis is taxed as ordinary income.

If you buy stock or an Equity Interest, your Basis in the context of our discussions so far is the purchase price of the stock or Equity Interest. If G2 purchases 100,000 shares of stock in Newco, LLC for $1.50/share, then their Basis is $150,000. If G2 then sells those shares for $5.00/share 20 years later, G2's gain is calculated based on the difference between the sale price and the Basis: $500,000 - $150,000 = $350,000. Absent other factors, the $350,000 is taxed at long-term capital gains ("LTCG") rates under today's current IRC.

In the course of executing a Succession Plan, G1, or the founder(s), usually has little Basis (absent, perhaps, a large acquisition that has not been fully expensed or depreciated). This means that as G1 sells their stock, Tranche-by-Tranche, the amount of the proceeds to the seller that exceeds the seller's Basis is taxable, usually at LTCG tax rates. The act of a G1 owner contributing all rights, title and interest in their Capital Assets into Newco upon setting up of the entity, does not increase or decrease the amount of Basis that G1, or any other owner for that matter, may have had prior to the contribution. Whatever Basis they had prior to their contribution is "carryover basis" in that what was previously the person's Basis in individually held assets carries over to be their Basis in the stock received for those assets.

The issue of Basis, as it impacts the Successor Team members, feels quite different. Focusing on just the next generation of ownership, G2s will buy their Equity and likely finance it with a conventional bank loan amortized over as long as ten years. The principal paid, as each installment payment is made, for this stock by G2 owners creates Basis—so while G1 owners typically have only nominal Basis, G2s and G3s may end up with hundreds of thousands of dollars, even millions of dollars of Basis. (Any interest paid is generally booked as an expense in the year of payment.) In the near term, the after-tax cost of the stock when G2s buy Equity from G1(s) is expensive, but the benefit is that when G2s and the rest of the Successor Team grow older, perhaps in an era of substantially higher tax rates, they will begin to sell their stock and be able to offset the proceeds against their Cost Basis.

Every shareholder of a Business engaged in a Succession Plan should put their Stock Purchase Agreements, Promissory Notes and related transaction documents, as well as copies of all business valuations or appraisals for each Tranche or purchase in a safe place and hold on to the documents for the rest of their lives. The IRS expects taxpayers to keep the original documentation for Capital Assets and investments; it uses these documents, along with third-party records, bank statements and any published market data, to verify Cost Basis during an audit. Similarly, specific records should be kept of Newco's assets at each buy in or buy out. If those assets have been depreciated, basis may need to be recaptured at ordinary income rates; however, if the assets at buy-in are no longer assets of the company, or Newco, having been replaced by other assets, recapture of basis may be avoided if complete records have been retained.

Calculating your Cost Basis is generally pretty straightforward, but something to always be discussed with your local tax advisor. In the course of a Succession Plan where growth fuels the buy-in process, the Plan and the hope is that the stock bought in Tranche One (T1) will double in size two or three times over during a G2's career. The offsetting Basis will be crucial when G2 starts selling their Equity to the G3 group of owners/investors. Basis is a principal factor in building a sustainable, multi-owner/multi-generational Business.

Think of this Lesson as the basics most Professional Service owners need to know. Personally, I learned the hard way when selling my own Equity Interest that the issue of Basis is much more complicated than a layperson may realize. Hold on to your paperwork and hire an experienced accountant on your Support Team.

LESSON NO. 31:
LEARNING TO LET GO

This Lesson is for my fellow G1s, and for many, this will prove to be the hardest Lesson to execute. I offer no judgment as to how you might go about it, just the shared experience of letting go of something that you've likely spent a couple of decades building, nurturing, worrying about, and enjoying. Letting go of the Business you've built is very hard. And even though a Succession Plan usually results in a delayed or slowed retirement, by choice, it doesn't change the fact that your Business will one day go on without you, and hopefully do even better.

Early in my business career, my CPA and friend told me that the art of building a great Business was learning how to make yourself irrelevant. At various times over the decades to follow, I ardently disagreed, then begrudgingly moved towards it as a point on the horizon, embraced it half-heartedly and then, looking back, finally accepted that advice. This is part of building a valuable, investable, sustainable Business. If what you've built cannot continue without you, it is not an investable Business.

The important point is that you, as the founder or one of the founders, should be able to control when and how your career comes to an end, even while (and especially as) the Business grows on the shoulders of your Successor Team and you work less and less as you monetize your investment. Good things to aspire to, but probably not enough to salve the wounds of not feeling needed or wanted any more in the Business you likely started.

Having made it over that retirement hill, or at least the letting go part, I can offer this. Don't look back—look forward and find a new passion and a new place to channel your energies. Don't stay in the business beyond the point where you're not needed and wanted. As a good rule of thumb, start by looking back on your typical work weeks over the course of your journey. Let's assume that, for instance, during your 50s, you typically worked five, 8-hour days (acknowledging that entrepreneurs work a lot more hours in the early years than that), or so.

When you start to consistently work, on average over a year, four 8-hour days a week taking into account vacations, sabbaticals, sick time, etc., reducing your office hours by 20% or so, then reducing your Equity Interest by the same amount, moving to an 80%/20%, G1/Successor Team ratio. When your work week declines to three, 8-hour days a week, reduce your equity interest by the same amount, moving to a 60%/40%, G1/Successor Team ratio, and so on. But when you get down to two days a week on average, or less, the Business and its new ownership team have to move on and do things their way as they have an investment to take care of. At two days per week on average, or less, it's probably time to let go and get out of the way, bluntly speaking.

I'm old school, or at least I was prior to having the work-from-home rules completely upended by that last pandemic. I'm honestly not sure what advice I'd offer to an owner who doesn't go in to the office but keeps working. If that process works for you and the Business, I think I'd just count the hours actually worked per week and apply the logic from there. (I do think the Successor Team members need to be on site more days than not.) At some point, I'd expect that the Successor Team leader is going to surprise you with a nice, big check and a "Thank you for all you've done" visit to your home office. Tell me and we'll both know.

The Lessons about using a Residual Equity Strategy (Lesson No. 26) and Learning to be Good Stewards of Ownership (Lesson No. 23), both might have some effect on your actual last day and how you handle the letting go part. Read and perhaps re-read those Lessons and have a heart-to-heart talk with your significant other and your business partners, look over your written goals, and adjust the Plan accordingly as a group. There's always a way to slow things down or to extend the process, but there is still going to be a last day for everyone.

Learning to let go is also about learning to trust the team you've built and mentored and respecting the direction they want to take the Business, which may be very different from what you want or expect. They'll likely have a large investment to recoup and they'll make changes as they deem necessary. That's their job. But it's not easy to watch. I found it was easier to turn away and walk in a different direction of my choosing. Businesses must evolve. Founders too.

LESSON NO. 32:
SELLER FINANCING VS.
BANK FINANCING

Not that long ago, seller financing was the norm in the Professional Services space for all Succession Planning transactions as well as most Exit Plans involving a third-party buyer. In its simplest form, seller financing, sometimes called owner financing, is when the seller (or G1 in our case) acts as the lender in place of a traditional bank. A common phrase used to describe seller financing is that the seller "holds the paper," usually in the form of a promissory note, or an earn-out arrangement, or both. *In the old days*, we said that "With seller financing, everything works!" And it did, and it still does, but it demands a very patient and risk-tolerant seller.

Over the past decade or two, things began to change very gradually. Banks started to consistently offer SBA, or Small Business Administration backed loans, for financial professionals, accounting firms, veterinarians, dentists, medical practices and such. This made sense because, from a lender's perspective, there aren't sufficient hard assets in most Professional Service Practices or Businesses to secure the loans (for a lender that wants to be over-secured). The problem with early bank financing support, as a part of the SBA requirements, was that the lenders usually required sellers (G1s) to sell all of their equity or assets and to effectively leave the business. Even the presence of a G1's ongoing, post-sale employment agreement was carefully scrutinized by the banks' underwriters and credit analysts. As a result, Seller Financing saved the day ten to fifteen years ago in the first Tranche or two and, on occasion, it still does.

Sellers, or our G1s, sometimes offer to carry the paper on a G2 loan(s) to earn the interest and to offer terms that, sometimes, banks simply cannot match. Sellers can also offer a variety of unique payment plans, such as interest-only payments for the first year or two, an actual Profit-Based Note as described in Lesson No. 21, a gradually stepped or increasing payment plan over the course of the loan, and more. Almost anything goes when the seller is willing to act as the banker.

Fast forward to the present day and many banks now are willing to offer conventional bank financing for five to ten-year terms at competitive rates, and for partial purchases of Equity as is common in the Tranche-by-Tranche Succession Planning process. With the evolution and improvement of banks' handling of Succession Plan and Exit Plan transactions, Seller Financing is less common today. Common Seller Financing scenarios today are when the amount borrowed is less than $100,000, when young, first-time buyers/borrowers are not able to meet a bank's minimum financial requirements, and for significant loans in an early Tranche. One of the common elements of all these Seller Financed loans is that G1 continues to come in to the office most days and is still an active participant in the Business.

On occasion, we've seen G1s offer a no down payment, no interest, deferred payment loan to help a younger G2 or G3 complete a first time buy in. Be aware that in such instances the IRS will impute interest on the transaction and can treat the imputed interest as income to the seller even if they haven't actually received any payments. This complicates the tax accounting and turns money that should be taxed as a capital gain to money taxed as income. At the very least, ask such questions of your local tax advisor before finalizing the financing terms; G2s and G3s will appreciate your kindness—the IRS does not. The Applicable Federal Rate (AFR), published monthly by the IRS, is the minimum interest rate that the IRS permits for private loans.

G1's motives in providing Seller Financing may not be completely altruistic as "the math" on this can be compelling (if one ignores the absence of that large, bank financed check at the beginning!). Over a period of up to ten years, during T1 or T2, the combination of principal and interest payments, plus G1's wages, and profits, and benefits, and stock appreciation (with G1 continuing to hold an Equity Interest as this part of the Plan unfolds) presents a lucrative package. Rather than a lump sum, the equity income and interest is spread out much more evenly over as long as a decade. With that, let's reconsider the concept of Shareholder Value that we explored earlier, adding in the Seller Financing component:

WAGES + PROFIT DISTRIBUTIONS + EQUITY INCOME + INTEREST INCOME + STOCK APPRECIATION

As always, a caveat or two. Most states, but not all, tax such income on an installment basis where you pay tax only on the money you actually receive in a given year. A couple of states accelerate the income stream for tax purposes even though you haven't been paid in full, so talk to your tax advisor. There is an obscure IRC provision on seller financed loans of $5.0M or more as well if that applies to you. Of course, this is an ever changing landscape and state revenue departments seem to be getting more aggressive. Also, even if the installment approach can be used, your income stream is subject to tax increases in the future, and again, with some caveats. For detailed guidance, you can refer to IRS Publication 537 on Installment Sales and talk to your local tax advisor.

To close this Lesson out, our standard advice is that Seller Financing makes sense when G1 is in the office, effectively in control, and in a position to watch over their collateral. The latter Tranches of a Succession Plan should always be bank financed if possible and practical. Let the bank be the bank.

LESSON NO. 33:
DRAG-ALONG RIGHTS AND TAG-ALONG RIGHTS

A Drag-Along Right, sometimes called a 'Come-Along' Right or 'Bring Along' Right, allows a majority shareholder (G1 for our purposes) who wants to sell 100% of the issued and outstanding shares of a Business to a third-party buyer, to compel minority shareholder(s) (G2s) to sell their shares in the Business on the same terms and at the same time. Tag-along Rights are often thought of as the inverse of a Drag-Along Right as these provisions are used to protect minority shareholders. In the event the majority shareholder decides to sell their shares to an outside buyer, Tag-Along Rights allow minority shareholders to participate in the sale on the same terms—basically, the minority shareholders cannot be excluded.

Succession Planning strategy and documentation often includes these rights in an interesting way. In Tranche One (T1), which typically sees a first time G2 buy-in for 10% to 20% of the Business's total authorized and issued Equity, Drag-Along and Tag-Along Rights are both commonly included in Newco's Operating Agreement or its Members Agreement (i.e., its Buy-Sell Agreement if drafted separately). Bear in mind that in the early years of a Succession Plan, where T1 is used as a kind of a testing phase, G1 still retains ownership of 80% to 90% of the Equity, and may well be the only Director on the Board. Frankly, no one is absolutely certain of the new partnership and its long-term viability in the first few years of T1. Accordingly, G1 has to hedge their bets and keep all options open.

In T2, the strategy starts to shift, especially if there are two or more G2's and they cumulatively own 25% to 30% of the outstanding Equity in the Business, or more, regardless of remaining debt service. When the G1's/G2's cumulative Equity ratio reaches 70%/30% or more, the G2s typically insist on having the chance and even the responsibility to be the buyers in case G1 decides to depart earlier than expected or if a triggering event occurs according to the Buy-Sell Agreement. A second buy-in and a second round of bank financing almost always causes this shift in thinking and tends to empower the Successor Team. A Continuity Plan works hand-in-hand with a Succession Plan.

In the Succession Planning documentation process, we recommend that the Operating Agreement and the Members Agreement in an LLC be drafted as separate documents, just as they are in a corporation. The Operating Agreement, like the Bylaws of a Corporation, are higher-level principles and governance provisions that really don't need to be, and shouldn't be, redrafted or renegotiated every year or two. The Members Agreement is different and may be amended more often as the Business grows and changes and as the Equity held by each generation of ownership increases or decreases. This is another case of applying commonly understood corporate attributes to the Limited Liability Company structure. A first-time buyer of 5% of the outstanding Equity usually doesn't request many changes to the Members Agreement; after the same buyer acquires another 15% of the outstanding Equity with a personally guaranteed bank loan, they will look at the Members Agreement very differently. The point is, Drag-Along Rights and Tag-Along Rights can and should be negotiated to reflect these ever present changes in the Business.

One of the negotiation points to be aware of in a Drag-Along Right is called the threshold level, which is used to set forth the percentage of shares or Equity needed to trigger the Right. This threshold is commonly around 60% to 75% of the authorized and issued shares. Other issues commonly negotiated focus on notice and timing requirements since the affected party needs sufficient time to determine the facts, figure out the best course of action, and probably obtain legal and tax counsel of their own. For context on these points, here is an example of the opening provisions of a Drag-Along Right:

> **Section 1.0.** *If one or more Shareholder(s) who, individually or collectively, own at least 75.0% of the authorized and issued shares (the Shares) of the Business receives a bona fide offer from a third-party to purchase 100.0% of those Shares, then such Selling Shareholder(s) shall have the right to cause each Remaining Shareholder(s) to sell all of their Shares to the same third-party on the same terms offered to the Selling Shareholder(s).*

> **Section 2.0.** *If the Selling Shareholder(s) described in §1.0 elect to exercise their Drag-Along Rights under this §2.0, then they shall deliver a Drag-Along Notice to the Business and each Remaining Shareholder at least 30 days prior to the closing of such sale.*

Practically, it is rare in the Professional Services space to see a Tag-Along Right exercised because the majority shareholder(s) will usually secure the highest price by procuring a sale of <u>all</u> the outstanding shares of stock of the Business, especially to a third-party. Unless that third party fashions a special deal to entice and reward the next generation owners, G2s and any G3s will cash out with G1 and then negotiate on their own with the third-party if they wish to continue their employment/ownership.

Drafting these rights is in the domain of an experienced business attorney, especially one who oversees Professional Service Business M&A transactions.

LESSON NO. 34:
THE DOCUMENT SET FOR
A SUCCESSION PLAN

In this Lesson, we'll inventory the typical set of documents that you will need an attorney to draft to support your Succession Plan. This list might seem daunting at first, but understand that this documentation/drafting process is not an annual event. In fact, once the entity is set up and the first Tranche is underway, there isn't much new documentation that will come along. The base templates will be in place and much of the mystery disappears. Formal business appraisals, of course, will be needed anew any time stock is bought, sold and financed. If a bank is involved, they will issue their own additional document set; we have not included these documents in the lists.

Starting with the new, Equity-Centric entity structure, whether a corporation or an LLC, using nomenclature appropriate to the form chosen (and even if you already have an entity set up, this document set will help you see what may need to add or amend to support this process):

<u>Newco, LLC/Partnership:</u>

Articles of Organization	IRS Form 8832 (Tax
Operating Agreement	Election Form)
Members Agreement	

IRS Form SS-4 (Employer Identification Number)

Consent Resolutions

Stock Transfer Ledger

Initial and Annual Reports

Trade name or ABN (Assumed Business Name)—if operating under a name different from that of the entity

Name Reservation Application

State and Municipal Registrations

Local Business Licenses

Employer/Payroll Registrations

There will be some variations given your city/county/state rules, regulations, taxes, and your intellectual property situation. While this list isn't exhaustive, it is intended to help you understand what it takes and why experienced, industry-specific local tax and legal counsel are an important part of the process.

S-Corporation:

Articles of Incorporation

Bylaws

Shareholders Agreement

IRS Form 2553 (to make a Subchapter S election)

IRS Form SS-4 (Employer Identification Number)

Consent Resolutions

Stock Transfer Ledger

Initial and Annual Reports

Trade name or ABN (Assumed Business Name)—if operating under a name different from that of the entity

Name Reservation Application

State and Municipal Registrations

Local Business Licenses

Employer/Payroll Registrations

If you elect the Hybrid Entity Structure (an LLC/Partnership with satellite Member S-Corporations or LLC/S-Corporations for each owner, described in Lesson Nos. 11 through 14), you can effectively combine the two prior lists. Of course, you may need an S-Corporation or an LLC/S-Corporation for each participating shareholder (G1s and G2s) with complete documentation for each. When filing IRS Form 8832 for an LLC, an election to be taxed as a corporation is required with the timely filing of IRS Form 2553 for each satellite Member LLC/S-Corporation.

Documentation for each owner to support Tranche One (T1) of a Succession Plan:

- Non-Disclosure Agreement
- Due Diligence Checklist
- A Letter of Intent or Memo of Understanding (optional)
- Contribution Agreement(s)
- Assignment & Assumption Agreement(s)
- Bill(s) of Sale
- Membership Interest Sale Agreement
- A Joinder Agreement (binding the buyer to existing governance provisions)
- Financing Documents (such as a Promissory Note and Security Agreement)

Documentation is important, and it is, for the most part, the final step in the Succession Planning process, at least per Tranche. Interestingly, each Tranche of the process ends with help from an attorney but each Tranche does not usually start with an attorney. The rules are simple but important: PLAN first, create a detailed pro forma spreadsheet to analyze the cash flow and compensation structure, then take your Plan to your tax counsel, and then, once approved and adjusted to the satisfaction of all owners (past and future), take the Plan to your legal counsel for complete documentation.

This entire document set is of the "forever" variety, especially for the next generation investors. Forget the basic rules about keeping records for 3 to 5 years. Safeguard them for life. I cannot tell you how many times I've gone back to my original documents, twenty years later, for some minute detail that matters for some obscure reason in our too complicated business and tax world.

LESSON NO. 35:
THE PLATEAU LEVEL
COMPENSATION STRATEGY

This strategy should serve to *connect a lot of dots* in the Succession Planning process as it attempts to shift the focus of new, next generation owners from that of an employee to that of a shareholder or Equity partner. The new G2 owners may come from within the existing Business as a key employee, a son or a daughter, or they may come from outside the Business as a Book owner being onboarded or merged in. These are a few of the many possibilities, but the most common.

As a first thought, no one buys in to ownership if it comes with a pay cut or what feels like a pay cut after debt service. At the same time, being a shareholder in an Equity-Centric, Professional Services Business is about so much more than just a paycheck. That is a bridge that needs to be crossed. To do so, let's revisit and build on the Three-Basket Cash Flow System in which, under Newco, LLC's new Profit & Loss Statement, cash flows into one of *three baskets* (see *Figure 17*):

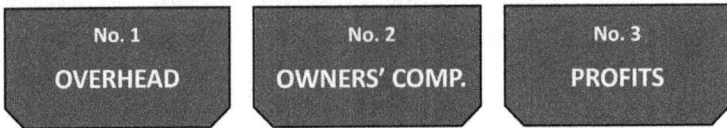

No. 1	No. 2	No. 3
OVERHEAD	OWNERS' COMP.	PROFITS

Figure 17

This Lesson centers on Basket No. 2 but in a different manner than we've explored in previous Lessons. Once a key employee or an outside, onboarding and investing owner comes into the Equity circle, they need to learn to shift their thinking from "I work for a paycheck and benefits" to "I work to build Shareholder Value (i.e., Wages + Profit Distributions + Equity Income (or - Debt Service) + Stock Appreciation). One of the best ways to help new, next generation owners learn to *think like an owner* is to use the Plateau Level Compensation Strategy, in one form or another. This strategy can also help the founding owners reset and improve Business profitability.

On day one of new ownership for a G2, this strategy starts by looking back on how much the new G2 owner earned in the past 12 months, or T-12 for trailing 12 months income. The spreadsheet modeling starts with this number, including base salary and any consistent bonus payments. Second, based on G2's anticipated role in the Business going forward, what does benchmark data suggest as a reasonable salary range for the work to be performed or the Officer's role to be held. Third, how much is the Business allocating to Basket No. 2, and for context, what do the G1 owner(s) get paid as wages for the work they do? New younger owners don't out-earn older, experienced owners. The process of figuring out the answers is not a mathematical construct, but rather taken from a set of guideposts.

The point is that once we narrow down "the number" or wage for the work that our new G2 owner is expected to perform, consider locking that wage number in place, along with that of all the other owners as well (who, hopefully are already using this strategy). To this end, let's say the ownership group (G1s and G2s) collectively agree that they will not change their base wages for three to four years; note that it is OK to pay bonuses to the smaller and/or younger owners, but I'd even start to get away from that within a few years. Cost of Living Adjustments can also be applied, especially as to the younger, newer owners who may be more cash flow sensitive—but base wages are frozen (see *Figure 18*).

Using this strategy as the Business grows, and especially as it grows, all

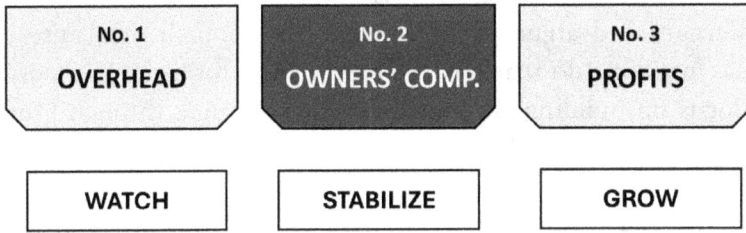

No. 1 OVERHEAD	No. 2 OWNERS' COMP.	No. 3 PROFITS
WATCH	STABILIZE	GROW

Figure 18

base wages through Basket No. 2 should remain relatively fixed and unchanged. There's a reason for this somewhat draconian approach. Under the *fun with math category*, think about what happens to the cash flow through your new or rebuilt P&L if the business continues to grow at 10% annually while one of the Business's largest expenses, the cumulative salaries of all the owners, remains fixed? Assuming Basket No. 1, General Overhead Expenses, remains relatively steady (acknowledging that growth will see expenses climb), and with Basket No. 2 not changing *by a handshake agreement*, then all new growth revenue, less expenses as the Business continues to grow, flows directly to the bottom-line of Newco, a Tax Conduit.

Depending on the Board of Directors' goals for profitability, this strategy can be used to quickly and steadily grow the bottom line in the Business's first couple of years, whether the goal is 15% profitability, 20%, or 25% or more. The fastest way to grow the bottom line is to fix the single, largest expense in place and grow the top-line. It seems simple, but it works—bottom-line thinking is what works.

No one wants to take a pay cut, and no new owner wants to work hard and grow a Business they've invested in and have a fixed, unchanging salary to show for it. So what is a new, next generation owner to do? And the answer is, grow the top line, watch the overhead, and take more money home at a lower tax rate through profit distributions (assuming an S-Corporation or an LLC/S-Corporation satellite Member is used), even as the share price grows tax free until one day it is sold.

One other major benefit to this Plateau Level Compensation Strategy is this—the ownership team avoids having to sit down every January or February and argue about who gets how much of a raise or a bonus. Just don't do that. Fix the base salaries for as long as possible and focus on building Business strength and value through growth, efficiency, and profitability.

With this basic concept in place, here is some practical advice that we've learned by doing it. It is OK to have a discretionary bonus pool that the Board of Directors can use to reward exceptional performance. This special, annual reward can certainly be used to augment the fixed, base wage structure, or elsewhere in the organization if warranted. There is a lot of flexibility in this approach and in your Business, once the concepts and the goals are understood.

LESSON NO. 36: OBJECTION!

This Lesson explores and addresses some of the common objections, or concerns, we hear from the founding owners (G1s) about the inner workings of a Succession Plan and G1's support (or lack thereof) to the process:

1) Sharing the Books and Records: As a part of every new, prospective next generation owner's Due Diligence regarding their prospective investment, a review of the Business's financial statements for the past three years is necessary, or at least recommended. The problem that arises is that many small business and sole owners use their cash flow stream as their own, personal *piggybank* where they write off a lot of *interesting* business-related expenses—no judgment intended as I did the same thing. These matters, and the full range of such expenses, are usually discussed only between the owner and their CPA or EA, and maybe a bookkeeper. Sharing or disclosing this information to key employees-turned-maybe-investors, along with the founding owner's annual salary and benefit package, is often a point of significant discomfort when first setting up an internal ownership plan.

Our advice on this front is to apply a previous Lesson and use the Three-Basket Cash Flow System to determine if the expense(s) in question should be categorized as a part of your Business's general overhead (Basket No. 1), or part of an owner's wage/compensation package (Basket no. 2). In many cases, owners in a valuable, profitable, growing business are (or should be) provided with an expense account as a part of their base compensation package. That's CEO level thinking. A monthly expense account starting at $1,000 to $2,500, depending on Business size and cash flow, allows each owner to use the Business to support their efforts and work-related expenses, no questions asked. Categorizing an expense, for instance, under "Owner's Expense Account" on the P&L Statement looks better to a potential investor than "Spa treatments at Annual Conference," or "Tesla Model S payments."

And don't abandon common sense. If your next generation shareholder begins with just a 5% stake with nothing down, maybe relies on Seller Financing and/or is not a revenue producer, share a copy of the valuation results and the basic income and expense numbers in a condensed fashion (easy for a bookkeeper to do) without every last detail. That should be enough for starters unless your forum state specifies anything that a shareholder is additionally entitled to receive as a matter of law. When your next generation shareholder(s) invest in a larger share of the Business, or make an investment of $150,000+, or so, they certainly need to see all the details of what they're investing in. This simply makes them smart investors which, in the end, is what you want and need. Use this planning opportunity to steadily improve and streamline your bookkeeping practices and prepare the Business for the next level. An increasing level of formality in terms of financial statements is a part of the process.

2) Next Generation Successors Have No Money: Unlike third-party buyers, who tend to be two to three times the size and value of a seller's Practice or Business, most of the Successor Team members do not have sufficient, liquid funds to pay for their acquired Equity, and most can only make a nominal down payment on the Equity purchase if that. But that's not the end of the story.

The Successor Team members offer something else and something more. First, they offer G1 the opportunity to stay in control longer and to enjoy the benefits of Shareholder Value (see the Glossary for a definition, or revisit Lesson No. 9, *Rethinking Ownership*

Compensation in Light of Shareholder Value). Second, the Successor Team of next generation owners brings to the table the benefits of time, energy, and the ability to earn and invest lots of money from their wages, profits and growing equity value over the course of a 20 to 30 year Succession Plan (from their perspective). Third, growth is a key to making a Succession Plan work for all involved. Next generation owners have the motivation to make a real difference and to help the Business value double, maybe twice or more, during their ownership journey as growth is what effectively pays for their Equity Interest. And as the Business grows, smartly, it should produce more profit dollars.

When all is said and done, the Successors will have plenty of money—they just have to learn to harness the machinery of the Business to get there. They have to learn to think and act as owners and there's nothing like signing a personally guaranteed promissory note with a 120 month amortization schedule to add a little spring to one's step early on Monday morning of the next work week!

To be fair, during the first half of the Succession Planning process (T1, and at least part of T2), the founding owner remains in control, does most (or much) of the ownership level work and worrying, and makes most of the money. By the second half of T2, and all of T3, maybe even T4, the tables start to turn. The Successor Team, led by the G2 owner(s), gradually moves into a position of control (if they've earned it, paid for it and have grown into proven leaders of a collaborative and collegial team). At some point, they will be expected to do most of the work with the founding owner still making most of the money (they are still likely the single, largest shareholder) through wages, profits and Equity sales. The Successor Team's reward comes later, and is substantial, if all the Plan's participants work together and take advantage of building on top of a solid Business model rather than starting their own Books or Practices from scratch.

3) I'm Paying Myself with my Own Money (Because the Next Generation Successors Have No Money!): To be certain, there is only one source of money sufficient to fuel the Succession Planning process, and that is the growing, profitable Business. The common objection on this front is that the profits shared with next generation owners would have been paid out and taken home by G1 level owners if they hadn't sold the Equity.

Selling Equity to the G2s but then giving them the profit dollars to pay for it sometimes doesn't sit too well with the selling party. And if G2 doesn't do their share after buying in, I'd be inclined to agree with G1 on this point.

We often counsel founding owners to remember that G1 isn't (or shouldn't be) granting stock or giving it away, which would then also include the related pro rata share of profits. G2 is making an investment. G2 is either going to sign a long-term, personally guaranteed promissory note as a non-controlling minority owner, or they're going to contribute all rights, title and interest in their Book to a Business that G1 is in almost total control of. Either way, that constitutes a substantial risk. Maybe the best way to look at this is that G1 needs to take a risk too and invest in the Successor Team. Every investment carries a risk.

G2 will eventually be responsible for revenue production and growth and as the Tranche-by-Tranche process unfolds, the G2 owner(s) have to pick up any slack as G1(s) slowly throttles back in terms of time in the office as they get older. At some point, certainly by T3, the cash flows of the Business, relative to G1, become "someone else's money". The best way to address this concern is to remind everyone that this is a career-length investment for all and roles and responsibilities will change over time.

4) G2 (or G3) Hasn't Worked Here Long Enough: Many owners ask when G2 should become eligible for an ownership opportunity. Said another way, "How long does a G2 prospect need to work for you before having an opportunity to become an equity partner?" Many Professional Service Businesses lean towards the seven to ten-year level of continuous service and employment at a given Business, borrowing a concept from at least the legal and tax professions. That works for many Professional Service Businesses, but a better rule of thumb is to make the ownership offer, or at least begin the discussions with a prospective ownership candidate, centered on the answers to these questions:

- What is your (G1's) overall timeframe and specific plan?

- When is your G2 prospect ready to make a career length commitment and sign up to a ten-year amortized, personal loan for this opportunity?

- How hard would it be to replace your key employee/G2 prospect if they left for a better opportunity or another ownership opportunity?

The point is, make your Business work for you as opposed to following some traditional or informal set of rules that may have little basis in fact. Ironically, one of the most common issues that prompts the start of the succession planning process occurs *after* several promising G2 candidates have left for *greener pastures*, as they say. To this end, make a Plan earlier than you need it and share the Plan with your G2 prospects. Let them know that Equity ownership is indeed on the table. Share the basic mechanics of the process. Make succession planning and business building over the course of generations part of your daily culture.

By way of a more direct answer, a preceding Length of Service (LOS) for a G2 or a G3 of three to five years is on the faster side of things, with four to six years probably being closer to the norm for most Professional Service owners. As a young lawyer, I remember being told that the unofficial *LOS rules* where I interned were seven to nine years, and if I didn't hear anything by end-of-year nine, don't bother asking! Rules are rules. Frankly, that was too long for me so I left and *hung out my own shingle*, and I had a lot of attorney friends who did the same thing.

If your talent is good enough, smart enough, and motivated to take the risk of being an owner, break the rules! It's your Business.

LESSON NO. 37:
WHAT IF MY SUCCESSION PLAN FAILS?

As your guide through these Succession Planning Lessons, it is probably clear by now that I am an unabashed optimist. When first starting my own Business, I used to get up every morning at 6:00 am and before leaving the house, I always polished my shoes, meticulously, and told myself "This is going to be a great day!" As many of you know from being entrepreneurs, during the first couple of years there can be a lot of bad days, and weeks, with too few paychecks while you scale the learning curve. But you have to stay positive and keep on trying. It's a part of the process.

Sometimes it helps to put the words on paper. Not all small businesses succeed. Not all stock goes up in value indefinitely no matter how hard you try. Not all investments work out—some can result in a complete loss of the invested proceeds as even the biggest investment firms add to their fine print, as a matter of law. Not all key employees should be owners. Succession Plans can help you build a more valuable, profitable, and sustainable business. They also can and do fail.

While I fully believe in this process and most every owner's ability to make it a success if they are determined, it is still challenging work. It takes time. You will need help. It takes commitment from all involved for decades. The 50 Lessons in this book? You'll learn even more on your own in the first Tranche alone.

The words in this Lesson are not intended as a caveat to all the Lessons in this book, just more of a reminder that even the best laid plans may not work out. Let's build from there and stare failure in the eyes.

So, you own a Professional Services Practice and you are working to put into place an Equity-Centric Business to support your Succession Plan. But along the way, each of the prospective new owners, even those who were key employee material with a solid Length of Service failed to work out. Either they chose not to make the investment or they did make the investment but then quit, were terminated, or defaulted. What have you lost? You might answer, "Some very good employees!" I can't argue with that, but if you're wondering if they're ownership caliber, my counterargument is that there is no better way to find out than to give them the opportunity and see what they do with it. The answer is not within your control.

You may not have succeeded in perpetuating your Practice, but you've likely made your Practice more valuable when the time comes for a sale, or Exit Plan, with a third party. Third-party or outside buyers typically own Businesses of their own and they value profitability and smart cash flow management. And learning to think like a share-holder or investor can only help your conversations with your own small business clients who want to share their experiences with you as a fellow owner. Many of the Lessons in this book are applicable outside the Professional Services ranks and can provide rock solid advice if you want to help your clients build stronger, more valuable Businesses. I witnessed this repeatedly with the financial service pro-fessionals I worked with.

Always an optimist, I suggest that the best approach is to plan well in advance, assume that failure is indeed an option, and maintain several good choices. Specifically, plan for both an internal Succession Plan as well as an external Exit Plan and solve for continuity issues in between. Apply the Three-Basket Cash Flow System even if you're the only owner at the beginning of the process and pay attention to profitability by taking control of overhead, owner's compensation, and top-line growth. Run it like a valuable, growing, investable Business!

Perhaps a better question to begin with is this: "What possibilities does this setback present?" Place the failure of your first option (a Succession Plan) in the context of your original goals. If your Plan fails, or said more correctly, if the founder(s) and next generation owners do not succeed in transitioning the entire Business over time from one generation to the next, an external sale or merger remains a distinct possibility—albeit at a higher valuation of your Practice in most cases. You may not have built a Business that lasts forever, but you will not and cannot fail to monetize a lifetime of work and leave your clients in a better situation than you found them.

In other words, if your Plan succeeds only in strengthening and growing your Practice and providing continuity protection for death, disability or interruption in your ability to run the business day-to-day, some particularly important tasks will still be accomplished. Just don't give up before you try.

Learn more and commit to at least the initial, important steps regardless of whether you make it to the finish line. Set up the proper entity and empower it with a modern, Business oriented cash flow structure with tax efficiencies—even as a force of one, that is beneficial. And create the "blueprints" for your Plan, perhaps a forward looking, ten-year pro forma spreadsheet, or even just a written, year-by-year layout of what needs to transpire over the same time period. Talk to your key employees about *that Plan*, and your hopes and dreams…and see what happens next. That is something that you do have control of.

LESSON NO. 38:
TAX EFFICIENCIES
IN THE SUCCESSION
PLANNING MODEL

A Succession Plan, and its underlying entity structure specifically, permit owners at the G1 level to build wealth and take money home at a variety of lower tax rates as compared to ordinary income rates under the current IRC. This makes long-term planning and Business building part of the value monetization process.

The concept of Shareholder Value, from a G1's perspective, directly applies to this discussion:

WAGES + PROFIT DISTRIBUTIONS + EQUITY
INCOME + STOCK APPRECIATION

As a sole proprietor or a single owner LLC taxed as a Disregarded Entity (filing one or more Schedule C's attached to your form 1040 in most cases), all the money that flows home from your Book or Practice, after expenses are deducted, is taxed as ordinary income. Effectively, we refer to this as a *two-basket cash flow model* with Basket No. 1 used for general overhead expenses and Basket No. 2 used for wages *and* profits which, in a sole proprietorship, are taxed at the same ordinary income rate.

When setting up an Equity-Centric Business to support a Succession Plan, we shift to a Three-Basket Cash Flow model (see Lesson No. 7), which becomes more impactful as the Business starts to make money from the efforts of others as well. With the table now set, let's talk about the tax efficiencies assuming that your entity structure includes an S-Corporation (this could be a basic S-Corporation, an LLC electing to be taxed as an S-Corporation, or a Hybrid Entity Structure which utilizes an S-Corporation as a satellite Member of an LLC taxed as a Partnership). This might be a good time to re-read Lesson No. 13, Entity Structuring Choices (An S-Corporation), for the mechanics and some caveats that may apply under city/county/state law depending on your geography.

In Tranche One, or T1, the founding owner(s) will receive wages for the work they do (at ordinary income rates), plus profits for the ownership they hold (at slightly less than ordinary income rates) after the first sale in T1, plus sale proceeds at long-term capital gains tax rates less any basis, even as the Business continues to grow with the help of the new, next generation owner(s). Stock appreciates tax free until one day it is sold and the value is realized. Those are four different and declining tax rates as money and wealth are created and realized. Of course, the ability to write off business expenses, perhaps both in the primary office and your home office, adds yet another beneficial layer. And there's more...

Over time, as the Succession Plan moves into T2 and T3, the assumption is that as G1 gets older, they will gradually work fewer hours in the Business. This assumption is based not only on observation and common sense but also on the need to forge a strong Successor Team. In a Succession Plan, the clientele of the Business, as well as the staff members, need to see the G2s gradually assuming more responsibilities. Spending a little more time out of the office and trusting and training the next generation owners to *keep their hands on the wheel* is a necessary part of the process. It is also an important benefit to G1 that doesn't show up on any spreadsheet.

As G1 slowly reduces hours worked, there is a strong tendency for

G1's wages (Basket No. 2 in a Three-Basket Cash Flow model) to plateau indefinitely and even, over time, to decline, sometimes offset by a stipend for their Director's role. This is why laying out the details of the Succession Plan cash flow over ten years is so important. In a growing Business, even as G1's wages plateau or decline in the last Tranche, G1's profit distributions should continue to climb, as well as their stock price since the G2s are using smart, efficient growth to fuel their debt service and investment in the Business. Note that the income stream at the highest tax rate to G1 is the first to be eroded; that's not a coincidence. G1 has other ways, and better ways, to get the money home!

Other possibilities include utilizing a Residual Equity Strategy to provide G1(s) with ongoing profit distributions as well as stock appreciation benefits, and Seller Financing to even out the cash flows to G1 and to add an interest component.

Every Succession Plan is unique and every Plan, over time, affords its founding owner(s) with a variety of options tailored to their individual needs as well as the Business and its investors. The combination of a founder working fewer hours while taking home more money at lower tax rates has to be considered by every owner as they think about how their story might end.

LESSON NO. 39:
YOUR CLIENTS GET A VOTE
ON YOUR SUCCESSION PLAN

Celebrate and champion this Business building and strengthening process with your client base from the very start of Tranche One. Your business clients can learn from you and *with* you. The benefits of a Succession Plan will positively impact not only your clients but their family members, friends, and business associates as well—which will support your long-term Business growth goals. A Business built to last is special, and it merits referrals of new clients from multiple generations.

As I worked full time in this profession for the past 30 years, there wasn't a week that went by that I didn't hear from one of my clients explaining why they felt they needed a Succession Plan. For those who were in their 50s, 60s or 70s, it came down to being repeatedly asked this question by their clients: "What happens to me, if something happens to you?" Granted, the need for the question and an appropriate answer depend on your Professional Services venue and whether you already work in a larger Business or you're a sole proprietor, but pro- actively solving for this concern and *thinking around the corner* is smart ownership. For Book owners, the best answer might just be a merger of interests using the Tax-Neutral Exchange process. At the very least, it is a 180 degree course adjustment.

As a G1, I hope that your answer, if you ever need one, and after reading the 50 Lessons in this book, will be something like this: "I'm glad you asked. I do have a Plan, a very good Plan. Let me tell you about it because you might want to do the same thing!"

A Succession Plan will help you demonstrate to your clients and colleagues that, whatever your Professional Service and line of work may be, you're invested in their future as well. Professional Services are like that. There are no boxes of widgets to be manufactured, sold and delivered by a faceless bureaucracy. This is a person-to-person delivery model.

Some of my past clients have related stories about how they proudly included in their company newsletters their G2's trek to ownership, their growing skills, their new title(s), if applicable, and their investment in the Business, which also says something important about the Business—it's worth being an owner of! Others hosted client appreciation meetings on an annual basis and made their recent Succession Planning steps a key part of that meeting so there would be no surprises in the years to come. The story of a Succession Plan becomes one of addition rather than subtraction as more leaders and owners are coming, than leaving through retirement. Still others introduced their new, next generation owners and used the opportunity to help nurture a new line of business oriented to a younger audience closer in age to the Successor Team member(s), who would then be the primary service providers, perhaps at a slightly lower or different price point. Lots to think about.

In addition, I have observed my previous Succession Planning clients utilizing this chance to address the Age Proximity Rule in the Professional Services industry. This rule suggests that senior owners usually serve clients who are within a 10-year age range of themselves. Rather than surrendering to an aging client demographic, why not reapply that rule with a 39-year-old G2(A) and a 31-year-old G2(B) in the equity ownership circle?! Consider this avenue as you celebrate your own Succession Plan and adapt your Business to serve multiple generations of clientele and maintain a strong, sustainable growth rate from one generation to the next.

Your Succession Plan also does something more, as it ensures that your talents, as the founding owner and entrepreneur, with years, perhaps decades of experience, are not lost. One-generational Books and Practices, the norm in the Professional Services ranks for many venues, witness an almost complete restart with each generation as the younger PSP's start their own Books or Practices. Building-in a mentorship aspect to a multiple-owner and multi-generational Business provides better services, and seamless continuity of those services, from generation to generation. Depending on your profession, which may have more or less importance, but it seems to me that having that attribute is a lot better than not having it. As you progress from entrepreneur to business owner, and then from CEO to mentor, celebrate it with your clients, for your clients. This is a good thing.

LESSON NO. 40: ASSEMBLING YOUR SUPPORT TEAM

Most Equity-Centric Businesses that successfully implement a multi-Tranche Succession Plan gross over $1.0 million a year, if not at the start, certainly early in the process. At that point, and beyond, most owners need a professional team around them, on an as needed basis, which includes the following:

(a) Accountant (usually a CPA or EA)

(b) Bookkeeper

(c) Business Attorney, and possibly a specialist Tax Attorney

These same professionals can help a founder transition their Book or Practice into an Equity-Centric Business, to later be joined by the additional following professionals in the design and implementation of a Succession Plan:

(d) Consultant/Succession Plan Designer

(e) Financial Analyst

(f) Appraiser

(g) Bank Liaison (or someone who's been with the bank awhile and knows how things work, like a Private Banker)

Collectively, this "group of seven" is your succession planning Support Team. After Tranche One, or T1 is implemented, most of the work by the Consultant and Financial Analyst will be done as well, leaving open the need for some fine tuning of your Plan over time as it evolves and you learn. Your Support Team might be local, and they might not be. In today's world, it is just as likely that you will work with an experienced Financial Analyst on the other side of the country—it really doesn't matter if they're good at what they do. The same is true of a business Appraiser.

Your Support Team, whatever their talent and experience level and regardless of where they're located, needs to understand and have experience with more than just your basic Business model. As a Professional Services Provider (PSP), it really helps to have an Accountant and a business Attorney that serve other clients just like you and in your specific line of work or profession. You don't want to be their largest client (as good as that may sound) or the first and only client in your specific field for your tax and legal counsel to practice on—and the only way you'll know is to ask the question. "Who else, like me, who does what I do, do you provide services to?" And then listen very carefully to the answer. Not all businesses are the same, and building an Equity-Centric Business with a Succession Plan will put you in an entirely different category and level of needed advice. Even the 20-year veteran accountant or legal counsel is unlikely to have much direct experience in your specific field and in supporting and documenting an actual Succession Plan.

In this day and age, I've found it necessary to also inquire whether the person I'm talking to, or interviewing, will be personally doing the work I need done or supervising an employee on their payroll. Ask it that way because, while it is OK to have a junior associate doing the legwork under a senior partner's experienced supervision (hopefully at a lower fee), more tax, legal and valuation services are being out-sourced to providers on the other side of the world. I get it that there are a lot of smart service providers out there on a planet with almost 8 billion people, but I'd rather not have my taxes or business appraisal prepared by someone on the other side of the world, no matter how smart they are. In any event and whatever you decide, it is good to know what you're dealing with and paying for beforehand.

Separately, ask your current and/or prospective Support Team members, or prospects, how many of their clients have second-generation businesses? Third generation? And, again, listen carefully. The Age Proximity Rule in the previous Lesson applies here as well—that most Professional Services owners typically serve clientele plus or minus 10 years their age. Younger Accountants and Attorneys may have no one that they counsel who are in their second or third generation of ownership, unless it is a G2 or G3 owner. That may not be helpful to you as a G1 owner. Something to think about.

Every Succession Plan I've worked on that has turned out well has involved a Financial Analyst. You just can't fake the math, and you cannot document the Plan without having a complete, detailed and forward looking spreadsheet of the Plan. This is not a requiem for determining who is most important on your Support Team; it's more about the order of things to come, and tax planning and legal documentation follow the analytics.

Let's talk more about the Financial Analyst as a member of your Support Team. In some instances, this person is a Chartered Financial Analyst, or CFA®, or individuals trained under or supervised by a CFA®, who can construct a ten-year pro forma that models a detailed Plan for the Business itself as well as each individual owner's *Shareholder Value* perspective. Note that this is generally not a CPA/EA function or skill set, and certainly not that of an Attorney. The Financial Analyst team member is tasked with modeling on a pro forma basis your specific variables using current and anticipated cash flow models, year-by-year, and Tranche-by-Tranche, accounting for all the owners or possible owner/investors along with debt service and tax impact, using projected growth rates, salaries, profitability levels, and much more.

Appraisers ultimately help you determine business value and produce an appraisal report specific to the purpose at hand; it is the Analyst who will help you determine the actual sales price of the Equity Interest—perhaps the appraised value, but perhaps not. This pro forma spreadsheet process, managed well, usually *is the Plan*. It is a persuasive document for the founder(s) and every member of the prospective Successor Team, even the other members of the Support Team. Understand that formally designed and modeled Succession Plans usually do not involve contracts for T2 and T3 that require an owner to sell, or a next generation owner to buy Equity at a predetermined time or price in the future. The final pro forma spreadsheet serves as a guide for all the owners and prospects and is readily adjusted as circumstances warrant over time. As a result, the spreadsheet can also function as an informal Term Sheet or Letter of Intent.

Once the pro forma modeling is finished (which can take months to complete given the detail that is needed and the many drafts it can take to craft a plan satisfactory to all involved), the next most important person on the team is your local CPA or tax advisor. The Financial Analyst and/or Consultant need to go over the Plan with your local tax counsel so that city/county/state/federal taxes are taken into consideration. At this point, everything from the entity structure to the compensation plan is considered in a tax context. Once your Accountant signs off, a business Attorney (usually with an M&A background) takes over and often works with a bank loan officer to coordinate and complete all the documentation for the Plan. Many PSPs, when first embarking on a new Succession Plan want to set up their entity as the very first step, which moves the Attorney's role front and center. My advice is to slow things down just a bit and make sure you have your long-term Plan figured out, along with the complete tax picture, before deciding which entity structure you actually need.

Careful attention needs to be paid to the legal process and an Attorney's job to zealously advocate for their specific client. If G1 and each of two G2s all *arm up* with their own, separate legal counsel to battle to the finish, it can be hard to come back to work *after all the dust settles* and work as collegial business partners. Another approach is to have the parties waive the conflict of interest and have one Attorney work for the entire group. This approach can work quite well with the right counselor.

Investment bankers and business brokers are worth mentioning, though not because they belong on your Succession Planning Support Team. These professionals are valuable should you decide on an Exit Plan instead. Investment bankers and brokers generally do not make money helping you design and implement a Succession Plan. Their goal is to help you find a reason to sell to an outside buyer, all at once, and for the highest price possible, and then to make that happen. That's OK, if that's what you want; just be sure it isn't because they want it for you.

One professional that I left off the Support Team list, or our "group of seven," is that of an insurance professional. I've learned over the years that this is a very specialized line of work, and really not about term life insurance policy sales even though that is part of a Continuity Plan. There is a lot more to consider on the insurance front and I'd urge you to set aside any preconceived notions about insurance sales agents. If one of the owners has an insurance professional who also happens to be a wealth manager and is a Certified Financial Planner (CFP®), by all means, invite them to sit at the table and add their specific planning and insurance expertise. This person should be able to add a perspective that is unique and valuable, and they'll make your Plan better.

LESSON NO. 41:
THE FALLBACK PLAN—SELLING
TO AN OUTSIDE BUYER

If for some reason a Succession Plan cannot be implemented or it does not work out in the long term, the fallback position should be what we defined back in Lesson No. 2 as an Exit Plan. In contrast to the incremental stock sales and purchases of a Succession Plan, most Exit Plans are structured as a single, comprehensive asset purchase and sale to an outside buyer. To be clear, the buyer's business, usually through its entity, acquires the seller's assets.

An Exit Plan sale is usually simpler and always faster when compared to a Succession Plan. It may even provide a higher valuation, or multiple of earnings (EBITDA) using a rule-of-thumb approach. An Exit Plan is also more complete for a seller looking to end their ownership—on the day before the transaction closes, the founder owns their Practice or Business. The day after the closing, an outside or third-party buyer is the owner and the assets will be absorbed into that buyer's Business. The seller's Practice or Business, technically and legally, comes to an end.

Although that may seem a bit abrupt, most buyers and sellers work together to position the transaction as a value-add for the acquired client base and, whenever practical, the former owner(s) and key employees are often retained by the buyer to help ease the transition process and provide continuity for years to come. For the selling owner(s), this route not only can result in a higher valuation, or sales price, than with an internal Succession Planning series of transactions, it also eliminates the responsibility to operate and staff an ongoing business. Payroll is now the buyer's responsibility.

The Exit Planning process should begin with a formal, written Term Sheet or Letter of Intent (LOI), often framed as a business letter with signature blanks for the offer to be accepted. An LOI provides the framework for the transaction and creates a time frame for due diligence and the completion or closing of the transaction. Typically, at least some due diligence has been completed in order to support the LOI which necessitates the execution of an NDA, or Non-Disclosure Agreement.

LOI's and term sheets are usually non-binding but there is a presumption under the law that both parties will work in good faith to reach a definitive agreement once they've committed to each other. The price and terms, along with any contingencies, should be recited in the offer. As with the purchase and sale of a home, if multiple offers are anticipated, the seller or seller's representative (often an M&A specialist or an attorney) should make every attempt to coordinate receipt of the various offers within a narrow time span so comparisons can be made and the best offer can be accepted. Once an LOI is accepted, the seller will be required to stop negotiating with any other buyer.

The LOI process will state whether the buyer wants to acquire the seller's equity or the seller's assets—it is usually the latter. When a buyer acquires a seller's Capital Assets (client list, cash flow, goodwill, any intellectual property, furniture and fixtures), the buyer is able to write off or depreciate most of the purchase price over time. In addition, the seller is able to sell their Capital Assets at long-term capital gains tax rates. This is one of the rare occasions when the IRC serves the interests of the buyer and the seller. In addition, the buyer avoids having to acquire the seller's liabilities and expenses unless it is purposeful to do so, as in the case of an office lease. Along with the tax benefits, these cumulative advantages, at least when compared to a buyer of stock or Equity, tend to result in the buyer being willing and able to pay a higher price.

Valuations for the purpose of an Exit Plan are usually market-based, or include a market-based approach, to take into account recent, similar sales and values paid. Most sellers have experience with a market-based valuation if they've ever bought or sold a house. A home Appraiser in the field of real estate will look to comparable transactions, or "comps," in the same geographic area to see what similarly situated homes were recently sold for. An Appraiser for a Professional Services Practice or Business can and should do the same thing if sufficient market data is available.

From the seller's perspective, they will be expected to support the transaction for some period post-sale, usually for six to twelve months to help shepherd the clients to the new owner's team. If the relationship between buyer and seller remains strong, an ongoing employment relationship may also be extended. This post-closing support role is important and to ensure that the seller(s) is well motivated, most Exit Plan transactions involve some type of a look back provision. This contingency, which should be fully disclosed in the LOI, often takes the form of an adjustable or performance-based promissory note, or an earn-out arrangement, or both. Be aware that an earn-out may be taxed as ordinary income when capital gains was the intended result, and vice versa, if improperly drafted.

If a founder, or G1, starts the Succession Planning process too late in their career to have more than one Tranche, another possibility under the Exit Plan umbrella is a complete sale of the Practice/Business to one or more key employees, or even a son or daughter. In most cases, these buyers will be nowhere near as strong financially as an outside buyer, but the transaction can be presented as an orderly transition from one generation to the next. The clients don't need to know the legalities of the transfer, only that they'll be able to continue working with professionals they may know and have worked with in the past. With G1 staying on to help for a year or two, it can be shaped to look a lot like an internal Succession Plan. And, using an asset purchase under these circumstances, the younger, less financially well-off buyer receives some especially important and needed tax benefits. Financing in these transactions is often a combination of seller and SBA-backed or conventional bank financing.

> **Quick aside:** Once a G1 sells an Equity Interest to a G2, whether a key employee, son or daughter, the tax code basically requires that any and all subsequent transactions continue in the same manner. In other words, G1 cannot sell 10% of their Equity and then sell the balance as an asset sale allowing the buyer to deduct or depreciate the purchase price paid on those assets.

Regardless of whether you sell to a larger, stronger outside business, or to a trusted employee, son or daughter, Exit Plans for a Professional Services Provider (PSP) are rarely all cash transactions. It is possible to receive full payment in a relatively condensed manner (i.e., one to three years), especially if bank financing is involved, but because the primary assets are clients who can vote with their feet, buyers have to be sure the seller can actually transfer the Capital Assets in full, or close to it, before full payment is delivered. For a seller who wants to cash out and not leave the business, the internal Exit Plan sale can make sense and can be shaped to benefit both sides of the transaction.

The take away from this Lesson is relatively straightforward: Monetize the value of whatever you have built and, if a Succession Plan is not possible, hand your clients off to the next generation through a sale—a proper way to finish the work you started. And, if it wasn't clear already, Exit Planning and Succession Planning are different but complimentary strategies.

In 2016, I authored a book titled *Buying, Selling and Valuing Financial Practices*, published by Wiley & Sons, which is available on Amazon. This book focuses on the Exit Planning process in intricate detail if you'd like to learn more about how asset-based, contingent purchases work, are cash flowed and taxed.

LESSON NO. 42:
APPLICATION OF
MINORITY DISCOUNTS

A minority discount is an adjustment to the Fair Market Value (FMV) of an Equity Interest due to a lack of control, a lack of marketability, and/or a lack of liquidity. In a Succession Plan, G2 and G3 owners will invariably become minority owners for at least the initial Tranche or two, and possibly for the duration of the entire Plan. Application of a Minority Discount to the Fair Market Value (FMV) of a G2's anticipated Equity Interest is a common discussion point.

A minority interest is for non-controlling ownership, commonly defined as owning less than 50% of a Business's authorized and issued shares. A Minority Discount applied to such an ownership interest in a small business reflects the notion that the stock may be worth less than its pro rata or proportional share of the total Business. Said another way, a G2's 10% share of the business may be worth less than 10% of the FMV of the entire Business because that interest lacks control, may not be marketable, and may not be liquid.

The Fair Market Value of shares constituting a minority interest is not set or specifically established by any law or rule. The applicable range of discounts, when applied to a Professional Services Equity Interest, is generally between 10% to 40% percent with every situation being unique. It is appropriate to calculate separate discounts for a lack of control, a lack of marketability, and a lack of liquidity with the cumulative total to be within the general range of 10% to 40%.

A discount, if offered, should be applied fairly and evenly. Consider that if a 10% interest in a Business is being sold to two members of the Successor Team at or at about the same time, the same valuation method and the same level of discounting (if any) should apply to each Equity sale. This issue goes beyond fairness if the entity in use is an S-Corporation which is limited by law to a single class of Equity. Selling the same equity at the same time to two different owners at different values could, arguably, create an issue for the S-Corporation owners and default them to C-Corporation status with very different tax rules.

Practically, especially in Tranche One, an Appraiser provides the answer and the logic as to Business value (usually FMV) and the Financial Analyst, who does the actual math on the transaction including after-tax costs and debt service amortization schedules, helps to figure out the price. As a general rule, in a Professional Services Business, price tends to lag value, especially in T1 (the price vs. value concept is explained in more detail in Lesson No. 18). The price of an Equity Interest in T1 is often effectively discounted from FMV to make the math work, a problem that solves itself over time with growth and additional Equity purchases. In T1, a 40% discount is rare; a 0% discount is not.

After T1 is substantially completed and if/when G2 buys in again, the FMV standard is typically applied and is determined without a discount or such a discount is ignored. In other words, in most cases, price equals value. Most of the Succession Plans I've consulted on over the years utilize only one minority discount, that in T1, and then never again regardless of whether the second and maybe third Equity purchase puts G2 in a minority position (i.e., three consecutive 10% Equity purchases). The problem being that there is usually only one seller of Equity, and the G1 sellers typically will not continually sell at a discount.

As the founding Business owner(s), it is entirely your decision whether to offer a minority discount. If you do offer a discount in T1, it is acceptable to never offer another discount in subsequent Tranches. There is no law or other requirement to do so. Understand that application of a discount is less an element of negotiation or a contest of willpower and more about making the math work for an after-tax buy in process by a younger, often financially impaired buyer. Very quickly in the Succession Planning process, this issue moves from theoretical to practical.

The counterpoint to a Minority Discount is a Control Premium, though generally this is not an issue in a Succession Plan with multiple members on the Successor Team. The notion behind a Control Premium is that if a minority interest is worth less than FMV due to lack of control, liquidity or marketability, then as a minority owner acquires enough stock to become a majority owner (i.e., more than 50%), they should arguably pay a premium above FMV on that purchase. It's a good argument but I've never seen it done in the course of a Professional Services Succession Plan.

Though most founders do not want to discount the sales price of their Equity, a Minority Discount can be beneficial if a founder is trying to grant or gift equity to a son or daughter, using the argument of lack of control and lack of marketability/liquidity to legally lower the price and help the buyer/investor avoid some of the tax consequences. In this sense, it works for both sides of the transaction though it must still be approved by the accountants who will file the related tax return(s).

Though the calculation of a Minority Discount is a technical and detailed professional process, it also has a very practical side. In sum, most G1s don't overtly provide a Minority Discount to a G2 or G3 prospective owner who wants to buy in because an Appraiser opines that they should. G1s apply the discount during the spreadsheet modeling if and when it is necessary because the Financial Analyst demonstrates the need. It simply comes down to the math and, bluntly in the words of a non-accountant, is an excuse for getting the numbers to work. If a discount isn't needed due to a given Business's strong growth and profitability, it usually isn't offered or provided.

Though it doesn't happen very often, a fast-growing, profitable Business might support G1's position that price should *exceed* value! At the very least, this argument should counteract the request for a Minority Discount. As a fellow or past G1 myself, that's how I'd handle it, if it made sense—absent an Analyst's admonition to the contrary.

LESSON NO. 43:
SECURITIES RULES AND
REGULATIONS

Early in my career, I served as an Enforcement Officer responsible for regulating the sale of securities at the state level. The term "securities" has a broad and complex definition but, for our purposes, suffice it to say that the Succession Planning process involves the sale of securities, or stock. Under some circumstances, a seller-carried promissory note may also constitute a security. Regardless, such sales even through an internal Succession Plan are regulated by all the states and the federal government.

Case in point, in every Operating Agreement I've prepared or seen prepared for every entity in every Succession Plan, this section is included in some form or fashion:

> Unregistered Securities. *The Shareholders or Members acknowledge and accept: (a) that the Shares of the Company have not been registered under the Securities Acts of the United States of America in reliance on an exemption from registration, (b) that the Company is not obligated to register the Securities, and, (c) that the Shares may not be offered, sold, transferred, pledged, or otherwise disposed of in the absence of an effective registration statement under the Securities Acts and applicable state securities laws or the Company is provided*

> *an opinion of counsel acceptable to the Company that such registration is not required.*

State securities laws are often called "Blue Sky Laws" and they are designed to protect investors against fraudulent sales and activities. One of the overarching goals of these laws is to ensure that investors receive accurate and necessary information regarding the type and value of a securities interest. While the laws vary from state to state, the basic framework of every state's Blue Sky Laws is to require registration of securities offerings unless the securities or the transaction is exempt.

The laws of each state typically have a lengthy list of exemptions, and the exemptions can be stacked so that more than one may apply. A common exemption offered by many states includes securities issued in connection with an employee stock purchase. Some states exempt sales to fewer than 35 purchasers in the state in a given 12-month period, or exempt sales to individuals who meet the definition of an accredited investor. Other states have *de minimis* provisions involving sales to 3 or fewer persons... but these laws are complicated and a qualified business or securities attorney needs to review the laws in your state given your succession plan, every time. This is typically not an arduous review process for an attorney experienced in this body of law. Also, many states have a Securities Section or Division where a regulator will take your call, listen to your questions, and provide some useful directions—one day a month, which was my job!

I'll also point out that there is not a single mention in the 50 Lessons in this book, until now, about the use of stock options or option contracts. For Professional Service Businesses of the size and type that are the intended audience, options are not necessary or commonly used, in my experience, and are not considered. Stock options take the securities regulation aspect to an entirely different level.

In the course of several thousand Succession Planning transactions, Tranches, and participants, I have never seen a succession planning transaction that was not exempt and that required registration in order to proceed. But that is not a safe harbor that you may rely on. You may come up with a slightly different Plan and change just enough about the process to step over some *hard to see* line, such as unintendedly using stock options.

So, talk to your business attorney who may refer you to a securities attorney. Regardless, you need to be absolutely sure on these issues before you sell stock in your Business to anyone. Generally, wait until your Plan is ready for documentation and add this item to your attorney's list of duties, issues, and documents to address. And, back to practicality, no one calls the securities regulators and complains because their investment performed beyond their wildest dreams! The investors who complain are those who are dissatisfied, lost money, whose employment was terminated, and/or who didn't receive all material information related to this opportunity, in hindsight.

LESSON NO. 44: ACHIEVING SCALE IN YOUR BUSINESS

As your Business grows and adds owners, the ability to scale it becomes increasingly important, and possible. Accept that it may well be the second generation who figures it out. If you're lucky, and smart about it, G1 and G2 owners can at least start the process together and develop a strategic plan.

With the benefit of hindsight, I've seen Successor Teams, time and time again, move forward on this issue. They have to…and they will. At some point, their investment depends on it.

Growth and scale are not the same things, and not every Professional Services owner understands that or is schooled on the nuances, so let's focus on it. In Lesson No. 10, "Grow, Grow, Grow!" we focused primarily on top line growth while watching overhead expenses (Basket No. 1) carefully with the goal of maintaining a certain level of profitability. But, by and large, growing the top line in a Professional Services Business usually means increasing the expenses as well, often proportionally. Scale is about growing the top line disproportionately to the general overhead expenses of the business. It usually requires planning, funding, and the right systems and processes, staff, technology, and partners. It can be extremely hard to do in a Professional Service model, but not impossible.

The issue of scale first arises when the strategies used in the past to grow your Practice or Business stop working, or at least stop working efficiently. Most entrepreneurs reach a point where they can't work any harder or longer, and they can't acquire and serve more clients. It feels like they need to expand, but any more growth feels impossible to sustain. At some point, there is just too much to do and not enough hours in the day to get it done. The common solution? Hire and train another person to do exactly what the founder and perhaps chief revenue producer does. And then owners do that over and over again.

The common result is that most Professional Service Businesses don't get more profitable, as a percentage of gross revenues, as they get bigger and generate more dollars in profit distributions. In the financial services and wealth management industries where I worked primarily, for instance, benchmarking data is clear that profits do not grow larger as revenues increase from $1,000,000 to $20,000,000— there is no material difference in overhead expenses or profitability for businesses in this range. They just get bigger.

Scale can be very elusive and I think the problem, especially in the Professional Services area, lies in entrepreneurial thinking, the very thing that helps every new owner survive in the early years of the new venture. As an entrepreneur, the first problem to solve for is revenue. If you can't make a living, your Book or Practice won't survive and you'll have to go get a real job! But over time, an entrepreneur's confidence grows and the myriad challenges and problems are solved using ingenuity, hard work, even some trial and error. At some point, however, problems like figuring out how to scale a business surpass one's basic entrepreneurial skills; working harder is actually part of the problem. I can attest to this from personal experience coming from a long line of workaholics and entrepreneurs.

Here are some suggestions to consider. First, growth is a common theme in a sustainable business, so apply the concept to the issue of adding scale. The challenge is immediate, but the solution is not—it will take time, perspective and skill. If your Business can currently grow at a 10% CAGR (Compound Annual Growth Rate), in seven years it will double its revenue flow. Start now and scale for *that business*. Who will you need? What needs to change? What's missing? Start answering those questions now and lay out a plan. Building for succession will provide a number of important guideposts along the way and require some new thinking.

Second, write down your goals and get specific—if you don't do both, nothing will happen. I'd go so far as to keep a journal on a project of this magnitude. Read. Learn. Hire a coach with a proven record in helping other Businesses turn the corner. Consider hiring the talent you may not have and bring in new and better thinking on this subject matter. Study other businesses, even from other professions and industries.

Third, marketing and sales are common pinch-points for one-owner Practices that want to grow into valuable, profitable, sustainable Businesses. This is because at the Book and Practice levels of ownership, the entrepreneur does it all and starts to honestly believe that they are the best and only solution to get more clients and produce more revenue. I know I did. Many Practice owners, forces of one, think the answer lies in this approach: "Find another one of me. I'm very good at what I do. And if I can't do that, then I've grown as large as I can." That is wrong and a self-fulfilling prophecy.

Hiring experienced marketing and sales professionals and arming them with goals and a budget dedicated to bringing in new clients and a high level of annual growth is a key step in allowing an entrepreneur to start to act and think like a CEO. This investment is inevitably a part of every investable and sustainable Business. PSP's rarely have any real training and experience in sales and marketing, other than being able to sell themselves. Why not allow trained and educated marketing and sales professionals to do what they do best for your Business? A common refrain that I like to apply to skeptics on this subject is to let leaders lead, let professionals deliver professional services, let marketing people market, and let sales people sell. When you consider it, it really doesn't make sense to ask a highly trained, perhaps licensed and regulated service provider to also sell and market themselves within a Business. Isn't the best use of a professional's time found in delivering professional services to as many clients as possible?

Fourth, building an Equity-Centric Business model provides unique tools to scale a business. Think back to Lesson No. 35, *The Plateau Level Compensation Strategy*. As the business grows, Equity can and should play a bigger part in the lives of more key employees and service providers. Base compensation (wages + bonus) as the reward work performed should yield to the benefits of Equity and Shareholder Value. Again, in a multi-owner, multi-generational Business, the cumulative salaries of the ownership team is one of the largest expenses a Professional Services model has, if not *the* largest. Stabilize owner's compensation for the entire team of owners (Basket No. 2), using profit distributions and stock appreciation in a growing Business as the reward and incentive, increasing profitability directly and indirectly. That's a big step in the right direction of scaling a Business.

Finally, when you benchmark against your competitors, if such data is available, be careful not to reinforce incorrect thinking—at this point in the 50 Lessons, you may well be contemplating building something vastly different from most owners have or will ever build. If you do, or benchmark against, what all the other one-owner, non-scalable, one-generational Practices are doing, you will simply learn how it is that everyone else is failing to build a valuable, profitable, growing and sustainable Business. The crowd isn't always so wise, or maybe you're looking at the wrong crowd.

You might note that scalability isn't listed as one of the attributes of an Equity-Centric Business. Not all Professional Service owners agree that it is necessary or even possible. I'd argue that bigger solves a lot of problems for Business owners and investors, but bigger isn't the same as better. Working towards scalability will make your Business better, in this generation or the next.

LESSON NO. 45:
SHAREHOLDER AND
DIRECTOR MEETINGS

Shareholders and Directors should make it a point to sit down, sometimes off site, sometimes together and sometimes as two separate groups, and meet once per quarter to talk about the recent past, the present, and the near and long-term future goals of the Business.

For each meeting, prepare an agenda and have someone take notes or minutes. Have the CFO, or the person in training for that eventual role, present the financial performance of the Business including its growth rates, overhead levels, and profitability along with estimates for the next twelve months. A review of the P&L and the Balance Sheet, including current levels of liquidity, should happen at every single meeting. In at least one of the quarterly meetings every year, talk about ownership and the Business's succession planning strategy, and perhaps review the original pro forma spreadsheet models and talk about expectations over the next five years, and perhaps longer. This will help to eliminate surprises between future owners, buyers and sellers.

These meetings present an excellent opportunity to help next generation owners learn how to lead and run a Business alongside their peers. It is also a good place for other owners to observe general competence, interest, enthusiasm, and attitude from meeting participants, which often involves non-owner presentations of information and materials. Who shows up on time (i.e., five minutes early at a minimum)? Who shows up prepared? Who doesn't? Who comes up with the best ideas, or solutions? These meetings are often one big laboratory!

During one meeting a year, invite the Business's legal counsel and, separately, the Business's tax counsel in to make a report on issues in each of their domains. Obviously, tax planning and tax obligations may involve the bookkeeper as well, making this one of the few times that the entire ownership team sits down, slows down, and listens and thinks together about these issues. Learn from the past, control the present, and plan for the future as a team, and leave your stock certificates at home.

Depending on the Business's growth rates, or lack thereof, plans for staffing and payroll should be addressed at least a year out, and further if the Business is growing fast. Staffing and payroll affect issues of general overhead, profitability, and scale. The founding owner(s) should take every opportunity to listen and evaluate, not just to talk and control the room.

As the Business grows and the founder or founding team gets older, these meetings are the time and place to have the hard discussions about *how the story might end* for each senior owner, what everyone's hopes, expectations and obligations may be. This is an opportunity to memorialize the thinking and to put into writing (using only meeting notes or minutes) what was said and how the Plan appears to be evolving.

After each meeting, issue minutes to all the participants. At the start of the next meeting, if not sooner, ask for corrections and comments. The meeting minutes don't create a contract, but if accurate, they provide a common platform to evolve the thinking and strategies of the Business and all of its owners and serve to memorialize the process over time.

These meetings are an excellent place to start to groom the various

Officers and their specific roles in the growing, evolving Business. Before formally naming or appointing a COO, for instance, select and treat a particular owner or key employee as responsible for at least some of the COO's duties and see how well they fulfill the tasks. Ask the acting COO, or CFO, to prepare and deliver readiness reports at each meeting…and then listen and observe.

During the first meeting each year, assign each owner the task of reading the current Buy-Sell Agreement or Continuity Plan and talk about any changes that need to be made or issues that are now just starting to emerge. Involving the corporate attorney in this meeting might also make sense.

The last point is that G1(s) need to help the Successor Team actually function *as a team*. Giving everyone time to talk, think, even argue or press a point during these meetings is such a great opportunity to grow and improve, and to learn how to communicate and work with each other, all with senior ownership present and helping as needed. Don't miss this opportunity even if you think you already have too many meetings!

LESSON NO. 46:
THE CHALLENGES OF
MULTIPLE FOUNDERS/G1s

It is not unusual for two or three owners of similar age to start a new business together. But in the context of a Succession Plan and/or a Continuity Plan, age in this context can pose a real challenge. Two or three founding owners who are all in their late 50s, all G1s, provide a lot of experience and financial strength, in most cases, but when it comes to being buyers, time is not on their side. Effectively, without next generation owners in the mix, such a Business has few, willing and able internal buyers at the G1 level. The ages of the owners are one factor in this discussion, with the amount Equity owned by each, the value per share, and their retirement horizons being the other key factors.

Let's set the table and deal with this situation. Three owners, G1(A) who is 56 years old, G1(B) who is 55 years old, and G1(C) who is 53 years old. Ownership is held equally. The Business has done well and its value is approximately $6.0 million. The youngest of the G1 owners anticipates retiring earlier than his or her colleagues, hopefully around age 62, but none of the owners want to work much past 65. This group has struggled to assemble and retain sufficient next generation/G2 talent and is not confident in a Succession Planning solution. As such, all three are willing to consider a sale to a third-party or outside buyer under the right circumstances when the time comes. There are two potential G3 candidates who show a lot of promise, though both are in their late 20s and neither have run a business before, nor even owned their own Book.

The founders of a Business, if documented properly, tend to be each other's continuity partners through a formal, Buy-Sell Agreement. If something happens to one of the owners, the remaining owner(s) are usually obligated to buy out and pay value to the exiting owner or their estate. Depending on the value of the Business and keeping in mind that most conventional bank loans carry five to ten-year amortization or repayment schedules, having one of two or three owners leave when the group is in their late 50s can be problematic, and expensive. Sometimes, there isn't much choice, or warning. Obviously, having life insurance in place as a possible funding mechanism is wise. The Business, as we've previously considered, can be the buyer and the borrower if necessary, redeeming the exiting owner's shares, but this serves to place any debt on the Business's Balance Sheet, decreasing its value until the debt is extinguished. Redemption also creates a lot of Phantom Income to each of the remaining shareholders through a Tax-Conduit on a pro rata basis.

From a Succession Planning perspective, the modeling process needs to take into account the anticipated and, as specifically as possible, the retirement timeframes for the three G1 owners. One possibility is that the remaining G1 owners want to work well into their 70s; another possibility is that they bring in at least one G2 who can effectively buy-in, worst case, through a Continuity Plan provision, if need be, or more directly; or they can sell the entire Business together via an Exit Plan on a collective timetable that works for all. If a strategic buyer can be found, the Exit Plan might be fashioned as more of a merger, with all three G1's then continuing to work for the new and larger buyer/company.

Selling a Business of this size to the two younger G3's is not practical. At this juncture, there is likely time for only two tranches and that is if the first Tranche (T1) occurs fairly soon. T1 transactions rarely exceed $500,000 in value, per sale/purchase, because the younger owners usually are not comfortable with a larger amount of debt and debt service on an intangible Business.

It is noteworthy that, in a previous Lesson, we recommended that regular shareholder and Directors meetings take place on a quarterly basis. The issue in this Lesson is not at all unusual, and it may have no resolution in terms of a Succession Plan, but how it all unfolds should never be a surprise. This issue is one that should be discussed regularly in those meetings starting ten years earlier. Maybe in that time a solution can be settled on and implemented, and maybe not. Maybe expectations and time frames for each owner need to be adjusted for the good of all involved. Maybe selling to a third party is the best answer; time will tell. But just letting time pass without any plan and seeing what happens is not a good strategy either.

Another interesting possibility is to attempt to merge a similar but smaller and younger group of owners into this larger Business and jump-start the Succession Plan with two or more G2's who have ownership experience and who will become immediate owners upon completing the merger. This *coming together* may be a statutory merger when the two entities are corporations, or it may be an asset contribution when the continuing entity is an LLC taxed as a partnership. Those are details best left to an M&A attorney once a strong mutual interest in finding a solution exists.

As G2(A) and G2(B), equal partners, merge their $2.0M valued Business into G1s' $6.0M valued Business, the new, post-merger ownership structure might look like this on a Tranche-by-Tranche basis (see *Figure 19*):

Within a few years after the merger, T1 should occur, with T2 about 5 to 6 years later. G1(A) and G1(B) can use a residual equity strategy as another possibility. G2(A) and G2(B) will not need a long-term bank loan to buy-in during T1, T2 and T3 because they have equity ownership via the merger with no debt to service and this will allow them to use up to 20.0% of the profit dollars, each, to pay for a 7.5% acquired Equity Interest (T1), and then 30.0% of the profit dollars, each, to pay for a 10.0% acquired Equity Interest (T2), and so on. This provides an acceleration effect using the Profit-Based Note theory covered previously and explained briefly in the Glossary.

		Post-Merger		T1		T2		T3	
		Equity Levels		Equity Levels		Equity Levels		Equity Levels	
G1(A):		33%		25%		10%		0%	
G1(B):		33%		25%		0%		0%	
G2(A):		17%		25%		45%		45%	
G2(B):		17%		25%		45%		45%	
G3(A)								10%	

Figure 19

On day one, post-consolidation, the Business is worth at least $8.0M and with a good, diverse team of owners in place, powered by strong growth, the Residual Equity interests of 10% each for G1(A) and G1(B) could be worth $1.5 million to $2.0 million over time, buying some patience in the planning process.

Obviously, a restructuring like this changes everything, for everyone. These aren't easy to do, and compatible, long-term partners are not easy to find, but they offer possibilities and opportunities that neither of the smaller Businesses may have on their own. It just might be worth striving for and hiring a headhunter to compile a short list of prospects and getting to work on it.

The other obvious solution is to sell the Business as a group of three G1s to a larger, third-party buyer or consolidator and build employment agreements into the transaction for the parties who aren't quite ready to fully retire yet. Practically, small businesses of this size have a tough time attracting private equity as an alternative. But even a non-sustainable Business in its own right, that is growing and profitable, will have suitors. Just remember to sell on the way up, as the Business is growing, and not on the way down; best to sell too soon!

LESSON NO. 47:
HOW TO MANAGE BUSINESS DEBT IN A SUCCESSION PLAN

In this Lesson, we will examine what happens when a new incoming Book owner brings along some debt with their assets, and we'll consider what happens when that new, incoming owner joins a Business that has existing debt on its Balance Sheet.

Most Professional Service Practices and Businesses have fairly clean Balance Sheets—many founders and entrepreneurs are debt averse, though debt used strategically can be an effective way to grow and strengthen a Business. The most common liabilities and debts we see include an open Line of Credit (LOC) with a substantial balance (i.e., $100,000+), loans to a shareholder, equipment loans, tax liabilities, pending or threatened litigation, refunds or warranty claims, an EIDL loan, an unforgiven PPP loan, debt from a recent acquisition of another Practice and, on occasion, the debt from buying out a previous owner via a stock redemption (where the entity is the buyer). We don't usually see all those debts on any one Balance Sheet, of course! Real estate may be in a separate but related company with debtors related to the going concern.

In my consulting work, I have also learned to watch for debt that does not appear on the Balance Sheet but lies in the expense section of a Profit & Loss Statement, such as a personally owned automobile, a plane, or even an Airstream® trailer (ostensibly used for meeting clients around the country). A good CPA can help sort these things out and put everything in the right place on your financial statements. Balance Sheet debt should be a contractual obligation by the entity, or Newco, LLC in our line of thinking, but sometimes small business owners assign business-related personal debt instruments to the entity without a formal Assignment Agreement being used. That might be OK if you're a force of one; once investors come along, the books and records need to be more carefully maintained, which is a good thing.

An open LOC with a balance is not at all unusual. On occasion, however, owners use the LOC to support an acquisition, to pay off more expensive debt, for personal use, or to buy out another owner's interest. Technically, these particular functions are not what a LOC is for. A line of credit is for emergency use, or for short term ebbs and flows in the cash flow rather than a long-term installment loan. To this end, banks can require that a LOC be "zeroed out" at the end of every year or at least once in a twelve-month cycle (which is a good practice regardless of the bank's preferences). Also consider using a LOC in the context of Lesson No. 27, *Maintaining Adequate Liquidity*—a good strategy when an investor, Appraiser, or banker are looking over your shoulder!

As a simple rule of thumb, debt on the Balance Sheet is deducted from the value of a Business dollar-for-dollar. From an Appraiser's or banker's perspective, there are various kinds of debt and there is a difference between short-term, medium-term, and long-term debt. Regardless, if I were an investor, a G2, I'd argue for a dollar-for-dollar reduction in value and not budge from that position because the debt service dollars will have a direct impact on the profitability of the P&L.

Acquisition debt is an interesting case for several reasons. On the one hand, acquiring a list and group of paying clients, the related cash flow, perhaps some tangible assets and goodwill makes the business more valuable, and often sends the three-year growth rate, or three-year CAGR soaring. On the other hand, the debt on the Balance

Sheet offsets much of the value of the acquisition in the near term. However, as the Business continues to grow and services the debt, and especially if 90% or more of the client base transitions and are retained, and synergies emerge, value will eclipse the debt fairly quickly. Add in the tax depreciation benefits of an asset sale/purchase as covered in Lesson No. 41, and the numbers look better, sooner, as well. It is not unusual to find acquisition debt on a Business Balance Sheet whether it originated there or was assigned to the entity.

Acquisition debt works differently when a Book owner seeks to merge into an existing Business, a concept we refer to as "onboarding" in Lesson No. 14. Applying the basic rule that debt offsets value dollar-for-dollar, most onboarding owners choose to hold any debt personally and to service that debt personally because this maximizes the value of the assets that they are contributing to the Business via a Contribution Agreement. The higher the value of the incoming assets, with no offsetting debt, the greater the amount of Equity the Book owner will receive. Equity brings with it a pro rata share of profit dollars and stock appreciation in the now larger, stronger Business, courtesy of the onboarded clients, cash flow and goodwill, and the addition of another owner to help run the operation and contribute to future top-line growth.

Pause for a moment and consider what we just laid out in the preceding paragraph. A new, onboarding Book owner is going to hold on to any Book related debt while contributing all of their Capital Assets into Newco for a minority ownership position. That is a significant risk to be sure. Why would a new, younger owner do that? The common answers lie in the benefits of joining a larger, stronger, profitable Business and having the opportunity to acquire a larger ownership interest in the future, using the machinery of a growing Business (i.e., Basket No. 3) to service the debt. Strong profitability and sustainable growth, along with a formal Succession Plan, are what will attract onboarding Book owners.

Similarly, when G2 owners acquire an Equity Interest from the founders/G1 owners, such debt is always personally held. As a result, the buyers build up basis over the course of several acquisitions. In some Equity transactions, stock redemption is used, which means the buyer is the entity itself, or Newco, LLC. Newco buys an exiting owner's stock, either from cash reserves or by borrowing the money from the bank where its accounts are held, and redeems or retires those shares, resulting in debt on Newco's Balance Sheet. The remaining owner or owners have no personal debt in this situation, and now own a larger percentage of the total authorized and issues shares because there are now fewer shares outstanding. In effect, this is anti-dilution. The catch is that dollars earned and used to service the debt by Newco usually cannot be expensed or depreciated, nor is basis gained by anyone, resulting in Phantom Income that is taxed to the remaining owners pro rata.

It is not unusual for the Consultant/Plan Designer, the Financial Analyst, the affected owners and their local CPA(s) to all get on a planning call to go over the spreadsheet modeling on issues that involve debt. Debt matters, but if well-managed, it can make your business stronger and more valuable in the long run.

LESSON NO. 48:
FAMILY MEMBERS ON
THE PAYROLL

During the succession planning intake process I conduct as a Consultant, one of the questions I ask is this: "Are there any family members currently on the payroll? And, if so, do those family members actually work in the business on a full time or a part time basis? And, if so, do they receive a compensation package equivalent to a non-family member?"

The answers don't matter much in a one-owner Practice, but it does start to matter when new owners/investors think about buying-in and they look over the Profit & Loss Statement. The good news is that there is almost always a workable solution for this particular expense item. A lot of Book and Practice owners have their spouses on the payroll, and that can bleed over into a Business as well. I'm all for making a business work for its owners but a Succession Plan adds in a level of formality and accountability, often in a good way.

One of the best things that can happen to a small business owner is to take on an investor, or two, as in next generation G2 owners. To be clear, at the Professional Services level, the assumption is that the investors will also work in the Business and be on the payroll, and if a license is required, they will have it or will get it. The investor mentality and the need for a return on that investment in the form of profit distributions and stock appreciation rights means every dollar counts and every person matters. Sometimes, this is exactly what it takes to help an entrepreneur make the leap from a *piggy-bank* cash flow operation to that of a valuable, profitable Business that is sustainable, and perhaps, scalable.

To better understand this issue, let's put our three cash flow baskets, from Lesson No. 7, back on the table one more time. To refresh your memory, Basket No. 1 is for general overhead expenses, Basket No. 2 is reserved for owners compensation, and Basket No. 3 is for profits. When the spouse of an owner is on the payroll, they usually get paid out of Basket No. 1. In an Equity-Centric Business model, they essentially are shifted to Basket No. 2 and tucked underneath their spouse or significant other, a G1 owner. In other words, G1's total wages for the work they do will include what they want or need to share with their spouse or significant other. This works well provided it does not compromise the profitability level of Basket No. 3.

To this end, one of the first things a Financial Analyst will do when modeling a Succession Plan is to create a base year P&L Statement using the trailing twelve months, a T-12 P&L. Performance ratios, used to track the changing levels of the Three-Basket Cash Flow System year-to-year, are projected based on anticipated expenses, growth and efficiencies. If this cash flow system starts out at 45/45/10, for example, changes will need to be swift and certain or the investment may not happen. If the cash flow baskets reflect a frugal business operation and the base year is around 50/20/30, all things are open to consideration and adjustment.

The general and good rule here is that, in a Professional Services Business, people on the payroll need to come in to work or, if one is working from home, put in a full work day. If a founder doesn't like that change as applies to just them, a good solution might be the Hybrid Entity Structure outlined in Lesson Nos. 11 through 14, which allows an owner to handle their own personal payroll through their private LLC/S-Corporation satellite Member, another reason this structure is popular with Professional Service owners. The other owners can do the same thing if they like. In addition, for professionals accustomed to more of a sole proprietorship approach, each owner's individually owned satellite Member LLC/S-Corporation restores many of these benefits outside of, or after the cash flows through the main equity-centric vessel, usually an LLC/Partnership. This might be a suitable time to reread the entity structuring lessons with added context.

Culturally, having spouses (and/or children) on the payroll of a small business with multiple owners is difficult, sometimes *even if* they work in the Business. The clock on their involvement immediately starts to tick upon G2's entrance. It has to. Don't blame the next generation owners. As smart investors, they have to learn to pay close attention to the bottom line and, accordingly, eliminate inefficiencies. That's a good thing. G2s who put their houses on the line for this career-length opportunity may go along with the founder's pleasures for a while, but lifestyle practices don't tend to last or warrant significant investment, or grow into valuable, sustainable Businesses.

In fairness, Businesses are built to take care of their owners and the owners' families in addition to employees and clients. The process simply demands more formality when investors and bankers look over things on a regular basis. Accept that this change is a part of the process of building a valuable, profitable, sustainable Business.

LESSON NO. 49:
EMPOWERING THE
NEXT GENERATION

The succession planning process will not work without the support and long-term dedication of next generation owners and service professionals. They are *the* key component. But they need some help to get the job done.

As I get older, I seem to start a lot of discussions with, "In the old days…" or "In my day…" So, let's start there. In the old days, G1s had to Seller Finance everything and everyone as part of a Succession Plan. They were the seller, the banker, the boss, the beneficiary. They could do almost everything to make the process work—except to make a G2 buyer want to be an owner! The next generation had to want it on their own, and, somehow, in a way that impressed their boss, banker, partner, and…the person they were supposed to replace and out-perform one day. That's a tough job. Almost impossible. But it worked more often than not. These were my training grounds.

One of the most enjoyable parts of the succession planning process for me is talking to G2 prospects and owners, and sometimes their spouses. For almost every G2, unless they've owned a Book of their own, this is a first time ownership opportunity. During these conversations, some of the commonly asked questions are these: Where does the money come from? What happens if this doesn't work out? Does our credit score matter going in? Or will this debt affect our credit score once we've bought in? What are the tax implications of buying this stock? But my favorite question is this: How will things be different in the office after we become owners? That's a great question.

My usual answer is usually something like this, and remember, we're talking about empowering the next generation. "On the day after you become an owner, you will need to come in to work at the same time (or maybe a little earlier). You will probably park in the same parking space. You will hang your coat or sweater on the same hanger in the same closet or coat rack. You will sit at the same desk and answer the same phone and do the same things you did the day before you became an owner, and you'll earn the same amount of money for the work you do. What changes and, hopefully, what improves is up to you and your fellow owner(s). This is a long-term investment." In other words, "Get back to work!"

In fact, from the perspective of a new, younger owner, there are more things that remain the same than change. Restructuring ownership compensation has little to no impact in year one on new owners. Profit distribution checks will, hopefully, be issued once per calendar quarter, or so, and it may take a year or two of strong growth for that cash flow stream to make an impact in a new owner's financial life, especially after debt service. Signing a promissory note and starting to service the debt is a wake-up call for certain. Still, it takes something more to think and act like a good owner. It takes experience and a good teacher!

G1 will need to delegate more and teach more and guide the new owner(s). A couple of suggestions here. A new G2 owner may not be ready or have earned an Officer's title and duties (such as COO, CFO, CIO, Senior Vice President, Vice President, etc.), but it is good to start to delegate some of those duties and see how it goes. (Take a look at the suggested write-ups for the Officer roles of CEO, COO and CFO back in Lesson No. 29—this is another reason I suggest clearly spelling out who does what in your documentation process.) If it goes well, delegate some more of the duties and responsibilities and allow each new owner to grow into the role they seem best suited for. If all goes well, one day they will earn the formal title. Encourage creativity and listen to new ideas, delegating the responsibilities and the workload to bring the ideas to fruition to the new owner(s). Learning to mentor and to stand aside, even as mistakes are made, is a set of skills G1 will need to practice and master as well.

There is a significant difference between how most G1s, or founders, became owners and how most G2s and G3s become owners. Most founders of a Professional Services Business bootstrap their way to growth and prosperity. The business grows by reinvesting the cash it generates. Most founders do not take on hundreds of thousands of dollars in debt when starting their new ventures, though it might feel like it when you sign a seven-year office lease and perhaps an equipment lease. But, more or less, you are in control. Next generation owners, as part of a Succession Plan, will have to purchase and finance their step(s) into ownership. That is a big commitment especially for a minority or non-controlling Equity Interest. And then they may well be asked to do it again (T2), and again (T3).

In the end, both generations have plenty of motivation to come in to work bright and early on Monday morning, and get things done.

LESSON NO. 50:
LOOKING BACK...
LESSONS LEARNED

One of the advantages that I promised to bring you back in the Introduction section as your guide through this process is a sense of perspective. I have been setting up, adjusting, watching and listening to our G1s and G2s and G3s as they progressed through Tranche after Tranche over the course of time. So, what commonly happens a decade or two later for those who embark on building a sustainable Business? How do their stories end? This is one last Lesson to learn from with the advantage of hindsight.

Acknowledging that most of my experience has come from the Professional Services ranks of financial planning, wealth management, and independent insurance professionals (with a few other PSPs added in such as a dental firm and an electrical contractor among others), this is how things have turned out so far.

About 40% of these Professional Service Providers stayed on course and the succession planning process worked more or less as designed and as expected. Two, or three Tranches at the most, was the norm early on because G1s often started a bit late (in their early 60s), with each Tranche launched about once every five years, supported by Seller Financing. More recent succession planning ventures have started sooner (with G1 at a younger age) and are still working through a two, three, or four Tranche process with each Tranche bank financed and the Tranches spaced out longer, and with less overlapping. Based on initial goals, G1s certainly appeared to retire later through a Succession Plan than with an Exit Plan, effectively retiring on the job. Most of the Lessons in this book are based on our observations of this group.

So, is that good? A .400 batting average would get us into the Hall of Fame. The salient question, of course, is what happened the other 60% of the time? Acknowledging that data collection is not always easy to come by years after an engagement, here is what I believe happened.

About 30% of the Succession Plans either failed years down the road, or never really got off the ground—we will talk more about the reasons why later in this Lesson—and then resulted in Exit Plans. This group chose to sell to a third-party or outside business that was larger and more valuable (about 2 to 3 times the size of the acquired Practice on average). The selling Practices that were able to shift to a bottom-line format and increase their profitability tended to sell for a premium. And this is truly where failure equals success, at least in a financial sense.

The rest found out that they started too late, or due to slow growth and lower profitability their Plan took too long to unfold. Some of the G1s did not like having partners, did not like giving up control or sharing the decision making, and/or struggled with hiring, training and motivating next generation talent. G2s sometimes bought in, and sometimes they looked at the pro forma spreadsheet modeling, took it home to discuss with their spouse or significant other, and passed. This group did not get started in terms of launching a Succession Plan; the process ended after a thorough exploration. Oftentimes, it seemed like that was the right outcome. I expect that some of these Practices eventually found a buyer and others took the attrition route, where the founders kept working and gradually the Practice wound down over time on its own.

The common struggles for all, in hindsight, seemed to center on finding the right people and enough of them to support the Plan and the Business interests, along with generating strong, sustainable growth over the course of the Plan. Interestingly, the family business model didn't seem to fare any better or any worse statistically, though when the second generation of family members succeeded and completed the buyout of the founder(s), they almost always brought in non-family members to round out the ranks of ownership and leadership shifting to what we call a family-like Business model.

I constantly read various opinions and cites about how few first generation businesses survive into the second generation and how even fewer survive into the third generation. Abysmal results? I'm not so sure. Perpetuating a Business, let alone running it successfully for twenty to thirty years, is hard! And a lot of this comes down to the skills of the business owner, capitalization, the ability to recruit and retain talent, geography, and competition—and, let's face it, sometimes a little luck. The skills it takes to run a growing business are hard to master for anyone in any line of work. Throw in a recession now and then and, well, our 40% success rate seems almost, admirable. The Lessons in this book work and that I know for sure, but I suspect that there are too many other variables in the process for the success rate to ever top 50% (of those who try). I think that's the right number and I hope that we see it across the Professional Services ranks.

So, for the half that wants to proceed, what's next?!

A CALL TO ACTION

Thank you for reading this book. My goal has always been simple: to help you understand succession planning at a very high level and to give you the information you need to take control of your future as a Professional Service Provider and business owner.

If you'd like to continue learning, ask questions, or schedule a free 30-minute one-on-one consultation, simply visit:

www.DavidGrauSr.com

Or, if you prefer, just scan this QR code with your phone camera:

By scanning this code, you'll go directly to a page on my author's website where you can easily and quickly set up a free 30 minute one-on-one appointment to confidentially talk about your specific situation and see if a succession plan makes sense given your circumstances. While on my author's website, you can also:

- ☐ Subscribe to my monthly newsletter
- ☐ Ask questions by email about your specific situation
- ☐ Access my blog postings
- ☐ Stay updated on future books and tools

You can also learn more by visiting The Stewardship Channel at: www.youtube.com/@DavidGrauSr , where I regularly post new videos on building a lasting and meaningful small business that improves the lives of everyone it touches.

For a G1 owner, that's enough to get off to a good start and to gain the necessary momentum.

Shifting audiences for just a moment, if you're a Book owner or a younger, next generation PSP and you've made it this far in this first book, hand a copy to the Practice or Business owner you might like to be a partner with and use it to start a serious conversation. For you, I have also written a second companion book (Acquiring Your Future Through a Succession Plan) specifically for G2 and G3 ownership prospects. This book will help you understand your opportunities and obligations in greater detail. Essentially, I wrote this book from the perspective of a thirty-something year old contemplating ownership.

In closing, this might well be the first generation of Professional Service owners to embark on building valuable, profitable, growing, investable, and sustainable businesses using a set of blueprints as we have described herein. Let's get specific about the Business you want, and build the Business you need, to get you to where you want to go. Your adventure awaits!

The End

PostScript: If you enjoyed this book, please consider leaving an honest review on your favorite store or book distribution center. I would appreciate it very much.

GLOSSARY OF KEYWORDS, TOPICS & CONCEPTS

Age Proximity Rule. This guideline suggests that clients and service providers (such as insurance professionals, financial advisors, doctors, therapists, or consultants) are often within a ten-year age range of each other, easing the processes of trusting, communicating, and understanding one another.

Balance Sheet. This financial statement provides a "snapshot" of a Business's financial position at a specific point in time. A Balance Sheet contains the details of a Business's assets (what it owns), its liabilities (what it owes), and the owners' equity, which represents the net worth of the Business.

Bank Financing. In a Succession Plan for a Professional Services Business, members of the Successor Team may use conventional bank financing for incremental purchases of Equity, or an SBA-backed loan for a complete buy out of the founding owner(s). Bank loans to a next generation Professional Services provider, or PSP, who wants to acquire equity and be a member of the Successor Team are amortized over five to ten years based on lending guidelines at a given bank. Compare and contrast Bank Financing to Seller Financing, also terms in this Glossary.

Basis. Basis (also referred to as "**Cost Basis**") is the amount of a capital investment in property for tax purposes. In most situations, the

Basis of an asset is equal to what you paid for it, whether with cash, debt obligations, or other property. In a Succession Plan, the Cost Basis is the starting point for calculating gain or loss on the purchase or sale of stock or Equity. If you sell Equity in a Professional Services Business for more than its Cost Basis, you will realize a capital gain. If you sell equity for less than its Cost Basis, you will realize a loss. If the Cost Basis has been depreciated, the amount between the original Cost Basis and the depreciated Cost Basis is taxed as ordinary income. See also Equity, a term in this Glossary.

Blue Sky Laws. State securities laws, also known as "Blue Sky Laws," are designed to protect investors against fraudulent sales and activities. One of the overarching goals of these laws is to ensure that investors receive accurate and necessary information regarding the type and value of a securities interest. While the laws vary from state to state, the basic framework of every state's Blue Sky Laws is to require registration of securities offerings unless the securities or the transaction is exempt. Federally, The Securities Act of 1933, The Securities Exchange Act of 1934, and The Investment Company Act of 1940 may also apply depending on the circumstances, subject to common exceptions.

Book. This term describes a one-generational level of ownership as a Professional Services Provider (also see PSP in this Glossary). One can own a Job or a Book; the synonymous terms describe the base model ownership structure as compared to owning a Practice or a Business. A Book revolves around just one person's talent, drive, and personality. This level of ownership describes as a single individual, usually a sole proprietor, who often works from an executive suite or from home and sometimes on a revenue-sharing basis under someone else's Practice or Business. The goal of a Book owner is primarily that of revenue production. Compare and contrast a Book to a Practice and a Business, also terms in this Glossary.

Book Building. This term refers to a Book owner who continues to own their own clients and generate revenue often while sharing space with the larger Practice or Business models.

Business or Firm. In the context of a Succession Plan, and as used in this book, a Business defines an enterprise that is not only larger and stronger than a Practice, a Business has multiple owners and multiple generations of ownership. A Business also utilizes a professional compensation system that supports strong profitability. Profit distributions, in turn, augment the compensation system for Equity owners, to service the debt resulting from a purchase of Equity, and to recruit, retain and reward next generation owners. Sustainability is the goal and a hallmark of a Business or Firm. Compare and contrast a Business to a Book and a Practice, also terms in this Glossary.

Buy-Sell Agreement. See Continuity Plan, a term in this Glossary.

CAGR (Compound Annual Growth Rate). A CAGR is a way to measure how much a business (or investment) has grown over a specific period. The calculation process requires only three inputs: (1) the beginning value, (2) the ending value, and (3) the time period. A CAGR takes into account the effect of compounding which means that the growth builds upon itself.

Capital Assets. In a Professional Services Book or Practice, the individual service provider owns the client relationships, the associated cash flow, any tangible property, and goodwill. Collectively, these are referred to as Capital Assets which can be contributed into an entity structure. This shift in who or what holds the assets and value is the first step in building an Equity-Centric Business. See also Equity-Centric Business, a term in this Glossary.

Closely Held Business. A closely held business is a private corporation or LLC that is owned by a limited number of shareholders or members. Shares or units of such a business are not traded on a public exchange and cannot be purchased by the public. In the case of a Professional Services closely held business, the regulated or licensed owners and/or service providers also typically work in the business on a day-to-day basis.

Continuity Plan. Often referred to as a Continuity Agreement or Buy-Sell Agreement (also known as a Shareholders Agreement in a corporation, or an Operating Agreement and/or a Members Agreement in an LLC), this is a written contract that provides for an orderly transfer of ownership, control and responsibility in the event an owner suddenly leaves a Business. Sudden ownership departures might be due to choice or through termination of employment, a partnership dispute, death, or disability. These professionally drafted agreements anticipate a variety of triggering events and then establish rules to determine who can or will buy the equity and how it is to be valued and paid for. Careful coordination of the Continuity Plan documents with the overall Succession Plan is vital.

Contribution Agreement. This is a legal document through which a sole proprietor or Book owner contributes all of their rights, title and interest into an Equity-Centric Business in exchange for Equity via the Tax-Neutral Exchange Process. See also Equity-Centric Business, Tax-Neutral Exchange Process, and Equity, also terms in this Glossary.

Control Premium. A Control Premium is the additional amount a buyer, or G2 in this context, might be willing to pay over the FMV of an Equity Interest in order to acquire a controlling interest in a Business. This reflects that there is value to an owner who can gain control over Business operations and decision making. Compare and contrast to a Minority Discount, a term in this Glossary.

Disregarded Entity ("DE"). A Disregarded Entity refers to one of the tax elections an owner can make after filing Articles of Organization to set up a Limited Liability Company, or LLC. A tax election as a DE allows a single owner to report their income federally, and in most states, as though they were operating as a sole proprietorship, albeit one with limited liability in certain respects. The taxing authorities then disregard the entity structure for tax reporting purposes.

Drag-Along Rights. If a majority shareholder (typically a G1) desires to sell the entire business to an outside buyer via an Exit Plan, Drag-Along Rights (sometimes referred to as a 'Come Along' Right or a 'Bring Along' Right) give a majority shareholder authority to compel the minority shareholders (G2s) to sell their shares in the Business to the same outside buyer and on the same terms. Note that the Continuity Plan may require a super-majority of one or more willing sellers. Compare and contrast to a Tag-Along Rights, a term in this Glossary.

Due Diligence. As used in the context of a Succession Plan, Due Diligence is the process of investigating and verifying information about a Business and an investment opportunity. A prospective buyer, or investor, will typically want to review the Business's financial statements, legal documentation, entity structure and meeting minutes, a stock ledger, tax filings, regulatory and compliance records, operational manuals, Business appraisals, liability and/or litigation issues, among other things.

EBITDA. This accounting term refers to earnings before interest, taxes, depreciation and amortization and is used to measure a business's overall financial performance. EBITDA is a metric that focuses on the financial outcome of operating decisions by eliminating the impact of non-operating management decisions and is used by investors and banks.

Equity or Equity Interest. In a financial sense, and as used in this book, this term means a share or unit of ownership in a company or Business.

Equity-Centric or Equity-Centric Business. This Business model serves as the foundation to support a Succession Plan. An Equity-Centric Business has five key attributes implemented over the course of a Plan:

1. A shift in value from one or more individual revenue producers, to Equity, in an entity structure

2. A focus on profitability as the measure of business value and success

3. Building a business that, in the eyes of the next generation, is investable

4. Generating consistent top-line growth, year-over-year, and

5. Building a multi-generational, multi-owner Business and achieving sustainability.

Equity-Centric means the owners and ownership prospects are focusing on the value of Equity in the Business and not on individual clients or building their own Book(s) separate from others involved in the entity.

Equity Income. As used in this book and as part of a Succession Plan, the term Equity Income refers to the proceeds paid to the seller of Equity in a given Tranche, usually realized at long-term capital gains tax rates, less any Cost Basis. See also Tranche, a term in this Glossary.

Exit Plan. This term refers to a complete sale of a Book, Practice or Business resulting from a transaction with either an external, third-party buyer or an internal buyer such as a key employee, or son or daughter. Regardless of who the buyer is, the commonality is that the transaction is completed in one step, usually an asset-based sale/acquisition as opposed to the incremental series of stock or equity sales that define a Succession Plan. Compare and contrast to a Continuity Plan and a Succession Plan, also terms in this Glossary.

Fair Market Value ("FMV"). FMV is defined by the American Society of Appraisers as *The amount at which a property would change hands between a willing buyer and a willing seller, neither being under any compulsion to buy or to sell, and both having reasonable knowledge of relevant facts.* FMV is a standard of value and is the most commonly applied standard in the context of a Succession Plan, but it does not necessarily result in the highest value of a given Practice or Business. Compare and contrast Fair Market Value to Intrinsic Value, Investment Value, and Synergistic Value, also terms in this Glossary.

Flow-Through Structure. See Tax Conduit, a term in this Glossary.

G1, G2, & G3. The term "G1" refers to the first generation of ownership, or the founder(s) of a Business. The terms "G2" and "G3" are used to refer to the second and third generations of ownership relative to G1's age, or the average ages of all the founders of the Business that are still actively engaged. Actual family generations are not required in this system; a gap of 15 years minimum between G1 and G2, and G2 and G3, etc., is usually sufficient to support sustainability in a Professional Services Business.

Hybrid Entity Structure or Hybrid Model. These synonymous terms refer to a common structure utilized by larger Professional Services Businesses often with valuations of at least $5.0M. The Hybrid Structure occurs when the operating entity for the Business is an LLC taxed as a Partnership and one or more of the owners each hold their interest in the LLC/Partnership through an LLC electing to be taxed as an S-Corporation. This is the most powerful and adaptive entity structure for a Professional Services Business because it offers the flexibility and fluidity of a Partnership with the tax savings of an S-Corporation, though it requires multiple entities to achieve these cumulative benefits.

Intrinsic Value. This standard of value refers to the value of a Business if sold to financial buyers, using private equity as an example. Intrinsic value refers to the perceived value of a Business in the eyes of a buyer who sees greater value than a market might ordinarily place on such assets. Value investors look for businesses with higher intrinsic value than market value; they see this as a sound investment opportunity. Compare and contrast Intrinsic Value to Fair Market Value, Synergistic Value, and Investment Value, also terms in this Glossary.

Investment Value. This standard of value refers to the value of a Business if it is to be sold to an investor or a corporate buyer; it attempts to consider the perspective of an investor whose purchasing decision necessitates an investment that can consistently generate a specific rate of return. This differs from Fair Market Value due to the differences in uses and investment objectives. Compare and contrast Investment Value to Fair Market Value, Synergistic Value, and Intrinsic Value, also terms in this Glossary.

IRC or Internal Revenue Code. The U.S. tax code, or Internal Revenue Code, is a body of law covering the federal tax laws in the United States found in Title 26 of the U.S. Code. The IRC is about 7,000 pages long; when tax regulations and official guidelines from the IRS are included, the total body of law is about 75,000 pages. In addition, each state has its own tax code.

Liquidity Discount. This discount from Fair Market Value, typically applied to a Closely Held Business, is a reduction in the value of an Equity Interest due to its limited ability to be converted into cash without affecting its market price. See also Marketability Discount, a term in this Glossary.

LOC or Line of Credit. A Line of Credit provides for immediate liquidity "on demand" with access to funds to be used whenever needed up to the limit of the Line. Unlike a loan which is best used for a onetime, fixed expense with installment-based repayment terms, an LOC functions more like a credit card.

LOS or Length of Service. This term is used to reflect an employee's time, measured in years, working for a Business or the G1 owner/employer. LOS matters because key employees, even sons/daughters, need enough time to prove themselves worthy as ownership prospects and enough time to decide if they want to make a career-length investment in the equity opportunity at hand.

Managers/Board of Directors. These synonymous terms in this book refer to those authorized to make management decisions for a Business. The structure used for a corporation, that of a Board of Directors, works equally well in an LLC in the form of a Board of Managers. This and other of the traditional "corporate attributes" are adapted for use in an LLC entity structure in this book. The powers of the Directors are set forth in a corporation's Bylaws or an LLC's Operating Agreement, each within the statutory structure of the forum state. Directors typically have one vote on key issues regardless of the amount of Equity they own, making this a unique governance tool.

Marketability Discount. This discount from Fair Market Value, typically applied to a Closely Held Business for which there is no public market or exchange, is a reduction in the value of an Equity Interest due to its lack of a ready market. This discount attempts to account for the difficulty in selling an Equity Interest quickly without affecting its price. Also see Liquidity Discount, a term in this Glossary.

Members/Shareholders. These terms are used synonymously in this book to refer to the equity owners of a Business. "Members" is a term used by a Limited Liability Company, whereas "Shareholders" is the equivalent term applied by a corporation.

Members Agreement. Often drafted separately from the Operating Agreement in an LLC in which a Succession Plan exists, this agreement serves as the Buy-Sell Agreement. Just as a corporation has Bylaws and a separate Shareholders Agreement, we consistently recommend in this book that LLC's draft separate agreements for the "constitutional provisions" of the business, vs. the buy-sell terms.

Minority Discount. This term refers to the economic concept that a partial, non-controlling ownership interest (less than 50%) in a Business, may be worth less than its pro rata share of the total Fair Market Value of the Business because the minority owner does not have the authority to direct or control the Business operations. The amount of a Minority Discount, if any, is typically determined by a professional Appraiser and is based on each individual set of circumstances.

Newco, LLC, or Newco. This is the generic term used throughout this book for a new (or existing and rebuilt) entity structure to be taxed and cash flowed as a Disregarded Entity ("DE"), a Partnership, or an S-Corporation. The working assumption is that Newco will be set up as a Tax Conduit or flow-through structure in order to support the individual investors and the Business's goals under a Succession Plan. See also Tax Conduit, a term in this Glossary.

Officers. On a day-to-day basis, it is the Officers, such as a CEO (Chief Executive Officer), a COO (Chief Operations Office), a CFO (Chief Financial Officer), or even a President and series of Vice Presidents, who make most of the meaningful decisions that move a Business forward and help it to grow and prosper. Officers in a Professional Services Business are usually, but not always, Shareholders as well. This term is used and applied independently of the requirements of many states, which necessitate having a designated President and a Secretary.

Onboarding. This term refers to the process in which an individual contributes their Book to a Business (which is typically structured as an LLC taxed as a Partnership) in exchange for an Equity Interest in the Business. See Tax-Neutral Exchange Process and Equity Interest, also terms in this Glossary.

Partnership. Used in the context of a tax election under a domestic LLC, this is the default tax structure when there are two or more owners, also called Members or partners. Profits and losses in an LLC/Partnership can be shared on a pro rata basis or as the owners determine and document in their Operating Agreement. An LLC/Partnership is a Tax Conduit or flow-through entity structure and provides the owners with limited liability protection in certain respects. See also Tax Conduit, a term in this Glossary.

Performance Ratios. See Three-Basket Cash Flow System.

Phantom Income. This term refers to income not physically received by an owner of a Tax Conduit entity but which is still taxable to the individual owner(s), usually on a pro rata basis. Phantom Income occurs when more income is allocated to an owner than is distributed to such owner. It can be created when a business redeems stock from an owner who leaves or retires or when a business pays a non-deductible expense, such as premiums for life insurance policies on the owners.

Plan. See Succession Plan.

Plateau Level Compensation Strategy. This strategy focuses on setting a relatively high level of compensation for each owner as the foundations for an Equity-Centric Business and Succession Plan are being set in place, and then "locking in" that level of compensation for all owners for three to five years at a time, or as determined by the Business's leadership. Since owners' compensation is one of the largest Business expenses, freezing that expense allows bottom-line profits to grow more rapidly. The result is that newer, next generation owners learn to focus on growing the business in an efficient, profitable manner in order to maintain their personal cash flow through a combination of fixed wages and growing profits. See Equity-Centric Business and Succession Plan, also terms in this Glossary.

Practice. As compared to a Book or a Business, a Practice is defined as a level of Professional Services ownership that is not only larger and stronger than a Book, its owner will have made the investment in office space, will have at least a small support staff and will have assembled the basic infrastructure (desks, computers, furniture, fixtures, etc.) to support growth. Practice owners tend to have a formal entity structure, commonly an LLC or a corporation taxed as an S-Corporation, even though there is only one shareholder, by definition. With strengthened foundations, time, and a good plan, a Practice can grow into a full-fledged Business with a Succession Plan.

Professional Services Business. The term "Professional Services", for purposes of the Succession Planning strategies referred to in this book, includes any Practice or Business whose core output is a service requiring specialized knowledge or skill and often requiring a professional degree, license, certification or registration. See Succession Planning, Practice, and Business, also terms in this Glossary.

Profit-Based Promissory Note. This term refers to a spreadsheet modeling process that isolates the share of acquired equity, such as 10%, to the same share of profit distribution dollars received from that specific, 10% equity acquisition only (ignoring any profit distribution dollars from additional equity that might be owned or purchased prior). In a series of overlapping equity purchases or Tranches, each purchase and each separate promissory note (Bank Financed or Seller Financed) stands alone in the modeling of the cash flows and amortization schedule. This strategy, if used, can take the form of a legal Note. See Tranches, Bank Financing, and Seller Financing, also terms in this Glossary.

Profit & Loss Statement, or P&L. Also known as an Income Statement, a P&L is a financial statement that summarizes the revenues, expenses, and any profits or losses remaining, for a specified period.

PSP(s). This acronym, used throughout this book, refers to a Professional Service Provider, or an individual who is capable, by way of licensing, education, or accreditation, of providing professional services to a client.

PSSP. This acronym, used throughout this book, refers to a Professional Services Succession Plan and is also used in the accompanying website supporting this book at **www.DavidGrauSr.com**

Residual Equity Strategy. This strategy refers to the ability of a G1, or founding owner, to continue to own up to 10% to 20% of their original shares or equity interest, after retiring and no longer participating in the day-to-day operations of the Business. This strategy allows G1 to continue to benefit from the flow of profit distributions, as well as stock appreciation rights until the residual ownership is sold. In addition, clients often benefit from the sense of continuity from one generation of ownership to the next. Owning residual equity is subject to regulatory constraints in various Professional Service venues.

ROI or Return on Investment. From a Successor Team member's perspective, as an investor, profit distributions and stock appreciation are considered being the *Return on Investment* for those who purchase an Equity Interest in a Business. The ROI must be sufficient not only to warrant the investment in a Business but also in the context of a PSSP, to service the associated debt of the buy in process.

Seller Financing. In its simplest form, Seller Financing occurs when the seller of an Equity Interest plays the role of the lender and *holds the paper* in a transaction—usually in the form of a promissory note. Sellers can mimic current conventional bank lending terms or can offer better terms within certain limits.

Shareholder Value. This concept refers to the cumulative benefits of being an equity owner. The basic formulas, depending on one's ownership level, are:

For G1 Owners: Wages + Profit Distributions + Equity Income + Stock Appreciation

For G2/G3 Owners: Wages + Profit Distributions – Debt Service + Stock Appreciation

Shares/Units. A "share" or a "unit" is a record or indication of ownership, or an Equity Interest. Though technically a share is a corporate term, and a unit is an LLC term, these terms are used synonymously in this book for simplicity and reflect the blending of corporate attributes into the more common LLC entity structure used by many Professional Service Businesses. Essentially shares and units work the same way, but it ultimately depends on the tax election that ownership makes as explained the entity structuring Lessons. See also Equity Interest, a term in this Glossary.

Statutory Merger. Covered by Internal Revenue Code (IRC), Section 368, as well as applicable state statutes, a statutory merger is a legal process in which one business, the "acquiring" business, effectively absorbs another business so that the latter business ceases to exist as a separate legal entity. In a statutory merger, all the assets, contractual rights, duties, privileges and obligations of the absorbed entity transfer to the acquiring and continuing entity by operation of law, which means that the transfer happens automatically. Shares of stock are exchanged in most cases so that the shareholders of the absorbed business are paid with shares of stock from the acquiring business.

Stock Redemption. A stock redemption occurs when a corporation (or LLC) buys back its own shares or units from an owner in exchange for cash, a promissory note, or other property.

Succession Plan or "Plan." As applies to the Professional Services space, a Succession Plan is best defined as a documented series of steps, or Tranches, designed to build a sustainable Business from which to seamlessly and gradually transition ownership, leadership, and revenue production responsibilities internally to a next generation of owner(s), referred to as a "Successor Team", whose individual members purchase Equity from a founding member in most cases. A Succession Plan is designed to support the evolution of the founder(s) roles and skill sets from entrepreneur, to Shareholder, CEO, mentor, perhaps even a residual equity owner.

Successor Team or Successors. A Succession Plan involves multiple owners and multiple generations of ownership, gradually assembled over time. The basic formula is this: G1 + G2 + G3, indicative of the next generations of owners, certainly including G1's children or other relatives if available and appropriate. This group of next generation owners are part of the Successor Team or are individually known as the Successors of a given Business. See G1 + G2 + G3 and Business, also terms in this Glossary.

Support Team. Most Equity-Centric Businesses that successfully implement a multi-Tranche Succession Plan gross over $1.0 million a year, if not at the start, certainly early in the process. At that point, and beyond, most owners need a professional team around them that includes an accountant, usually a CPA or EA, a bookkeeper (often part-time), and a business attorney. These same professionals can help a founder transition into an Equity-Centric Business. This initial and basic Support Team will need additional professionals in the design and implementation of a Succession Plan, to include a Consultant/Plan Designer, a Financial Analyst, an Appraiser, and a banking liaison. An independent insurance professional may also be an important member of this Support Team. See Tranche, Succession Plan, and Equity-Centric Business, also terms in this Glossary.

Synergistic Value. For appraisal purposes, this term refers to the value of a business if sold to a strategic buyer who might place additional value on the business due to the synergies that can be exploited by the combined firms. Synergistic value may emanate from increased revenue and/or lower expenses, additional territories or larger marketing footprint, the new or combined services that can be offered to both client bases, or some combination of all of these, thereby increasing the acquiring firm's income and cash flow.

Synthetic Equity. This umbrella term refers to the ability of a Business to provide key employees with some of the economic benefits of ownership without actual stock or Equity changing hands. Common Synthetic Equity plans may include phantom stock, stock appreciation rights, a profits interest, or a significant bonus that pays out only at the end of an employee's career based on the Business's value or success, among others. Synthetic Equity is something less than an Equity Interest with all its attendant benefits and obligations, and it is something more than a base wage plus a bonus.

Tag-Along Rights. In the context of a Continuity Agreement or Buy-Sell Agreement, Tag-Along rights protect minority shareholders. In the event the majority shareholder decides to sell their shares or units, Tag-Along Rights provide minority shareholders the option to participate in the sale on the same terms and conditions as the majority shareholder; in effect, to "tag along."

Tax Conduit. With conduit entities, such as a corporation electing to be taxed as an S-Corporation, or an LLC taxed as a Disregarded Entity (DE), Partnership, or S-Corporation, the entity itself does not pay taxes federally and in many states. Instead, all income or loss of that Business flow through to the shareholders, pro rata, who report these earnings on their own income tax returns. As with many of the tax laws and supporting rules, exceptions are commonplace at the city, county and state levels. A C-Corporation, in contrast, is not a tax conduit and is considered to be a tax payer.

Tax-Neutral Exchange Process, or "TNE." This process describes the most common type of "merger" between Professional Service

Providers, usually occurring within an LLC taxed as a Partnership. IRC §721 allows for a tax-neutral exchange of assets for Equity in entities taxed as Partnerships, and under certain circumstances, IRC §351 allows for a TNE of assets for Equity in entities taxed as S-Corporations, rather than a formal, statutory merger. See Onboarding and Equity, also terms in this Glossary.

Three-Basket Cash Flow System. This simple, rudimentary, but effective cash flow model is used to convey some important Equity-Centric Business building strategies, compartmentalizing incoming revenue flow to a Business. Basket No. 1 is for general overhead expenses of the Business, Basket No. 2 is reserved for owners' compensation, and Basket No. 3 is for everything that is left over, or profits. The general idea is this—overhead is the cost of running the Business and encompasses all expenditures except for the owner(s) salary. Basket No. 2 is for the owner(s) annual base salary, or wages for work performed. These two "baskets" serve to acknowledge that everyone, including and especially the owner(s), must be paid for the work that they do, but not all the revenue after overhead is paid should be allocated to the owner's salary. Balancing the cash flow in an appropriate, tax efficient manner between these three-baskets, or categories, helps to make a Business valuable, profitable, and investable. See also Equity-Centric Business, a term in this Glossary.

T-12. This term is shorthand for "trailing twelve months" of revenue flow.

Tranche(s), and T1, T2, T3. A typical Succession Plan design takes into account the value of the Business, G1's estimated time to retirement, the business growth rate, profitability, and, of course, the talent and ages of the G2s or prospective owners, among other things. From these inputs, the overall estimated length of the Succession Plan is divided into a series of Tranches, or significant steps. Most Succession Plans have at least two to three Tranches, which are denoted by the terms **T1**, **T2**, and **T3**. If a Plan starts when G1 is in their 40s, age-wise, the Plan might have four or five Tranches. See Business, Succession Plan, G1 + G2 + G3, also terms in this Glossary.

NOTES:

NOTES:

NOTES: